GARDEN ROCKERY

Rockery and water (page 164).

Frontispiece

GARDEN ROCKERY

HOW TO MAKE, PLANT AND MANAGE IT

BY

FRANCIS GEORGE HEATH

EDITOR OF GILPIN'S *Forest Scenery*
AUTHOR OF *The Green Gateway*, *The Fern Paradise*, *The Fern World*
Our British Trees, *The Fern Portfolio*, *My Garden Wild*
Tree Gossip, *Autumnal Leaves*, *Sylvan Spring*
Sylvan Winter, *Our Woodland Trees*
Burnham Beeches, *Where to*
Find Ferns, *Peasant Life*
The English Peasantry
etc.

WITH FORTY-FIVE ILLUSTRATIONS

LONDON: GEORGE ROUTLEDGE & SONS, LTD.
NEW YORK: E. P. DUTTON & Co.
1908

PREFACE

THE object of this little volume is to please and interest every one. It may be supposed that this is a very ambitious object. On the contrary, it is a very modest one. Those catering for public amusement and instruction give most pleasure who demand the smallest toll in the shape of study and trouble. Most people like to be easily amused. Life nowadays is so strenuous, and bread-winning, and other of the more important occupations of men and women, require such an expenditure of mental and physical energy, that there is none left to devote to recreation which involves a lot of preliminary study and preparation.

An expert and accomplished botanist said to me not long ago that he did not believe in "royal roads" to the study of plants. I replied: "Well, then, I suppose, if your life and fortune demanded an immediate visit to Paris, you would not dream of acquiring, rapidly, just as much of the language of that city as would enable you to go over and transact your business, but would insist on spending at least a year in mastering French before you started!"

The name of the lovers of gardening is Legion; but how many would indulge in the fascinating pastime if a condition-precedent were a thorough knowledge of botany—which requires a lifetime?

I believe that "a little knowledge" is *not* "a dangerous thing," but is, oftentimes, a very delightful thing! and I am going to show the worn and worried man, or woman, of business how to obtain a maximum of enjoyment with a minimum of preliminary attention and consideration.

There is no garden, however large, there is no forecourt or backyard, however dark, small, and miserable-looking, that cannot be improved and brightened by the introduction of a larger or smaller bit of rockery. There are plants that will live and thrive in the most dismal and depressing of shady corners; and the owner or occupier of dwellings to which such shady, dismal corners are attached—whether or not he is interested in what is called "gardening"—is bound to be refreshed and comforted by the addition to them of something fresh and green!

Every human being is, consciously or unconsciously, a nature lover! The human brain, the human mind, cannot help being pleasurably affected by God's sunshine and God's green growing things, and by all the sensuous colours and perfumes and tastes of the beautiful vegetable world.

Rockery is the most delightful and suggestive of all garden adjuncts; for it is reminiscent of the most exquisite of country scenes; it is a microcosm of mountain and valley, calling up to the eye and to the ear the crystal flash of running water—the loud melody of the roaring torrent, or the dreamy "gurgle" of the flowing brook.

How to produce this microcosm of the bold crag and the soft splendour of the gently-undulating hill-side is the object of the succeeding chapters.

FRANCIS GEORGE HEATH

SILVERTON.

CONTENTS

LIST OF ILLUSTRATIONS

GARDEN ROCKERY

I

THE GARDEN

PERHAPS in the whole of our language there is no word whose meaning is more elastic than the one which heads our first chapter. A garden is a place where plants are cultivated by man, in contradistinction to one where they grow wild. Strictly speaking, it means an enclosure (of any kind) which is first cleared of its natural wild growth and then replenished with such a selection of plants as the cultivator may prefer.

A garden may be simply a small pot, or box, filled with earth and some little plant or plants, or it may extend to thousands of acres, stretching away as far as the eye can see in every direction, and comprising specimens of almost everything contained in the vegetable world.

It will be interesting, perhaps, in view of the rapid growth during the last year or two of the taste for nature-study, to advert to the present writer's explanation, penned more than a quarter of a century ago, of the reason for the origination and extension of the love of gardening. He wrote: "The world, as understood to consist, not of so many cubic miles of matter, but of so much flesh and blood, and so much brick-and-mortar work—the populated or residential, as distinguished from the physical or natural world—is continually increasing. Towns are getting bigger, and populations are growing denser; and though natural resources give few signs of falling off, the struggle for existence is becoming keener. The town, being of man's making, is, like all man's works, imperfect. It is, in fact, of all human constructions the most imperfect; and citizens, by a natural and uncontrollable instinct, have always turned from it, on every opportunity, towards ' the country.' The early institution of ' the garden ' furnishes proof of the ancient existence of this feeling, which has grown with the growth of cities, and is stronger in the present day than it has ever been before. Of the various expedients adopted in modern times to give pleasure to urban populations, and to relieve the tedium of city life, there can scarcely be one which is more delightful, in every way, than the institution of city gardens. The love of Nature, which is innate in most people, has had less and less opportunity of indulgence as our towns have grown larger and larger, until city life and country life have become two distinct phases of existence. But as the augmentation of the number of human dwellings in any particular place has caused the country to be pushed, so to speak, further and further away, the love of Nature has, on the part of those compelled to live within the lines of bricks and mortar, become more and more intense in proportion as the absence from natural objects has become more prolonged. If, however, city people cannot always visit the world of nature existing outside their own, they can bring near to themselves the objects of their admiration. And it is undoubtedly this longing for communion with nature that has led to the institution of 'the garden,' which, in whatever age, and under whatever conditions it has existed, has always been established with one object, or rather with one desire, namely, the growth or cultivation, as adjuncts to the dwelling-house, and for purposes of beauty or use, of the vegetable productions of the earth." *

Gardening, indeed, may be defined, in a phrase, as the domestication of plants; and this domestication is very much less—than in practice it used to be—the distortion of plants from natural to viciously conventional forms. The Romans practised the hideous art—so called—of topiary, and considered it the highest form of gardening art. It consisted in the clipping of plants to make them assume the shapes of birds and animals.

* "My Garden Wild."

Gilpin was probably the first prominent writer, towards the close of the eighteenth century, to correct a taste which, even then, was prevalent; and his protests against the practice of topiary had considerable influence on the public mind; but bad customs often die hard, and with the almost entire disappearance of the monstrosities of topiary—for it lingers even now in some places—the eccentricities of modern horticulture came in; but these are happily now giving way to the increasing fondness of the votaries of gardening for natural methods of cultivation. How these can best be pursued it will be important to point out in the next chapter.

II

MICROCOSM OF NATURE

THE garden should be, what it very seldom is, a microcosm of Nature. As this little volume is intended to be eminently practical, let us say at once that it is not proposed to suggest, in the management of a garden, æsthetic impossibilities.

In a lecture which the author gave not long ago, by request of the Devon and Exeter Gardeners' Association, at the Guildhall of the famous cathedral city, the chairman, a local magistrate bearing a name widely known in the horticultural world and head of a large firm of nurserymen,* remarked, in reference to the subject of the lecture—"Trees, Flowers, and Ferns"—that whilst he and most of the audience were more familiar with the practical

* Mr. Peter Veitch, J.P.

side of the subject, that is, with the spade and fork and hoe, the author of the paper for that night was going to give them a little of the poetry of gardening.

There is a great deal of poetry in the subject; but as there is well-recognised "licence" in this as in other poetry, it is intended, in these chapters, to use it in recognising that art may modify nature, but only to the extent of selecting, from the great host of plants which crowd the vegetable world, such smaller or larger individuals as may fittingly adjust themselves or accommodate themselves to available gardening space.

It might be contended that if the natural disposition of plants is to be blindly followed one might take a piece of garden the size of a common, heath, or wood, and place in it exactly what is contained in those places, including a considerable proportion of mere grass: but there is nothing artificial, or opposed to the genuine promptings of Nature, in making a selection of plants to grow under domestication, according to the predilection of the individual cultivator. The vicious practice is to subject the selected plants to unnatural conditions of growth in order to produce unnatural features: to force the single blossom into the double form; to make the naturally white flower blue, red, or yellow; to compel the blue, red, or yellow flower to become white. Nature's variations in form and colour are endless and should suffice for the most exacting horticultural taste, without the display of cunning efforts to alter her wise disposition of form and colour.

Nature endows certain plants with a vigour of constitution which enables them to overcome others in the struggle for existence; and where large numbers of the same species are crowded together in confined spaces cramped and dwarfed forms are the result. It is assisting, not opposing, the efforts of Nature to afford garden specimens that the cultivator may select for his study and amusement more space than they ordinarily secure, in a wild state, for their development. Leaf, blossom, and fruit in wild plants enormously vary under improved conditions of growth. The pinnate, or once-divided leaf, becomes bi-pinnate and tri-pinnate, or twice and thrice divided, when the plant has more room to spread and a greater abundance of the moisture of air or soil and a greater quantity of leaf-mould, from which the particular plant's food is extracted. At the same time the blossoms will be larger in size and richer in colour, and the fruit more juicy and luscious. Under the same natural conditions the small herbaceous plant will become a shrub, and the shrub will develop into the nobler proportions of a tree. The small ferns of our temperate region would become tree ferns in the tropics; and it is the same throughout the vegetable kingdom.

The author, many years ago, in "My Garden Wild," expressed the opinion, to which in spite of any opposition he still adheres, that "Nature, left alone, can and does produce fruit which no skill of horticulture can emulate, although the conditions of its production are not such as can exist in the immediate proximity of a region of cities. We may venture to believe that although chemistry was unknown to our first parents, and although pruning and grafting were unnecessary, and 'hothouses' and the institution known as 'the greenhouse and conservatory' still undiscovered, Eden was, nevertheless, a paradise, and yielded food and fruit not, at any rate, inferior in 'quality' to that of our own times—assuming that Milton's description is only approximately correct:—

'With mazy errour under pendent shades
Ran Nectar, visiting each plant, and fed
Flowers worthy of Paradise, which not nice art
In beds and curious knots, but nature boon,
Pour'd forth profuse on hill, and dale, and plain,
Both where the morning sun first warmly smote
The open field, and where the unpiercèd shade
Imbrown'd the noontide bowers; thus was this place
A happy rural seat of various view;
Groves whose rich trees wept odorous gums and balm,
Others whose fruit, burnish'd with golden rind,
Hung amiable (Hesperian fables true,
If true here only), and of delicious taste.'

And on

'Another side, umbrageous grots and caves,
Of cool recess, o'er which the mantling vine
Lays forth her purple grape, and gently creeps
Luxuriant.'"

III

WHAT IS ROCKERY?

IN the sense intended here, "rockery" is *not* the aggregated abomination called "clinkers," a vitreous compound obtained from gasworks: it is *not* a structure made up of large or small sea-shells cemented together, often seen, but utterly out of place in gardens: it is *not* a pile of lumps of coke disguised to look like genuine stone by being first wetted and then sprinkled with Portland cement, although this contrivance may be adopted or Portland cement itself—mixed with sand to the extent of two-thirds of the bulk—may be wetted and made up into lumps in imitation of irregularly-shaped pieces of stone, if it is quite impossible to obtain the last-named substance. Rockery is *not* lumps of brick—although that may be utilised if broken into irregular shapes in the absence of the genuine material; nor is rockery a mixture of tree stumps and miscellaneous pieces of stone. Where stumps of wood are employed a warm and sheltered asylum is at once formed for myriads of small insects which, naturally, look upon the plants immediately surrounding them as placed there for their use and enjoyment; as, in fact, an easily-accessible storehouse of food. To watch them is to afford one of Nature's most interesting object lessons; but if the cultivator of a garden is not an all-round naturalist, he will prefer to let our insect friends—or foes, according to the differing lights in which they may be regarded—go elsewhere for their "daily bread"; and he can quite innocently and naturally, without destroying life—an operation which is very properly repugnant to many people—place lime or sprinkle soot around his favourite plants as a sort of notice to the hungry insects on the principle of "Friend, we do not want thee here!" We have heard of kind-hearted owners of gardens who, on discovering a snail engaged in the—to it—congenial occupation of lunching off the leaves or blossoms of a favourite plant, have lifted the small creature and, in the gentlest possible way, " heaved " it over the wall into the adjoining garden of a neighbour; but this is a kind-hearted course of proceeding which is very " bad form "—so far as the neighbour is concerned —and by no means to be recommended.

The best answer to the question " What is rockery ? " will be given to those who will take the trouble, when they have the opportunity, of noting how Nature makes her rockeries and plants them. The evolution of the planted natural rockery provides a most interesting phase of natural history. There are two principal methods: one produced by volcanic upheavals, the other by the " weathering " of exposed rock. The volcanic upheaval causes fragments of all sorts of shapes and sizes to be flung on to the earth—at lesser or greater distances from the place of upheaval—and the " weathering " causes blocks to be dislodged from solid cliffs in every conceivable variety of shape. The influence of rain and wind continued during hundreds of years produces what may be called rock soil—the aggregation of minute fragments, in soft heaps gathered into a thousand and one stony angles, of the prostrate masses. Upon these, more or less "hungry," little heaps certain bold and hardy vegetable seeds and spores fall and germinate. They spring up into forms of beauty, propelled by the magic—the wonderful, mysterious, and, to our finite minds, incomprehensible power of growth—producing leaves, stems, blossom, and fruit; and then, having ripened and cast the latter—the seed, or reproductive atoms for future generations—they die, and atmospheric influences reduce them to the elemental substances of which they were composed. They form, in brief, what is called "leaf-mould," an inert inorganic or dead substance, but a substance, nevertheless, instinct with vital food for the sustenance and development of their successors. These go through the same wonderful and beautiful process ; and, in time, there is produced an appreciable accumulation of vegetable as distinguished from rock soil. Other plants, more exacting in the matter of nutritive soil, tempted by the richer and richer accumulations in the rocky " nidus," are induced to grow and flourish in the same spots ; and thus in time the bare rock is clothed with verdure.

But the " weathering " process may take place on the open surface of huge rocks unaffected by volcanic convulsions ; and soft angles will be formed where accumulations of leaf-mould from the plants that grow there (in the way already described), augmented by wind-borne contributions from elsewhere, will, in time, produce the exquisite garniture which oftentimes turns bare rock into a dream of verdant beauty.

IV

WHAT STONE TO USE

FOR the framework, so to speak, of a garden rockery, whatever the size, position, and slope of the ground, it is important to employ natural stone; and resort should only be had to other substances when it is found absolutely impossible to obtain stone. As already explained, pieces of coke plunged in water and then rolled in Portland or other good stone-coloured cement, or well sprinkled with cement so as to conceal the actual material which is being used, may do as a substitute for the real thing; but then no moss or lichen, which largely adds to the charm of natural stone, will cling to the surfaces, and the spores of these delightful "accessories," as they may be called, will find no "nidus" for their germination and growth.

There are four kinds of natural stone which may be considered the best for the purpose. These, in the order of their appropriateness, are sandstone, limestone, Kentish rag, and granite. The porousness and soft exterior of sandstone render it most desirable, because it speedily acquires a mossy coating, and offers a holding for the roots and rootlets of many rockery plants; and ivy—one of the most delightful of creepers—will cling to it. Limestone and Kentish rag also make excellent material; but granite, being the hardest of all four, whilst very handsome in appearance is not so responsive to the affectionate clasp of tendril or rootlet—although the author has seen most luxuriant masses of the beautiful filmy fern—both *Hymenophyllum tunbridgense* and *Hymenophyllum unilaterale*—clinging, in dense masses, and completely carpeting the upper sides of huge masses of granite in moist regions where those beautiful ferns abound.

When the stones named cannot be obtained from the quarries or seaside foreshores, they can often be had from builders' yards. The blocks of stone least useful to the builder are the best for garden rockery—the misshapen, but picturesque, lumps—those are not available for many of his purposes, and are quite useless to him when they are in the soft porous condition most suitable for the garden rockery. Builders have continually to pull down old walls and other structures, and what they are unable to use on the spot for rebuilding they cart to their yards on the chance of finding some use for it.

Besides builders there are the "contractors" for road-making and miscellaneous "contractors," who do a good business by selling building material for any purpose; to the builder himself, when of use to him, or to the occupiers of gardens for edging of "borders" or grass lawns. Contractors who obtain large quantities of stone for road-making have to submit to the selection from their consignments made by the foreman of the road contractors, and it is customary, in some parts of the country, to throw discarded blocks—

discarded because of their softness—into the hedge-bank, from which they are picked up sometimes without permission and appropriated by farmers to mend hedges with, in gaps made by cattle ; and they do service for thorns or other hedge " fencing." These are the sources from which the garden rockery maker may obtain his material.

V

SOIL

NEXT in order of importance to the framework of a garden rockery comes the question of soil, as both stones and earth must be decided upon and obtained before the work of construction, to be dealt with in our next chapter, can be commenced. As a rockery will consist, if of large size, of a number of what may be called "compartments," and if of small size, of what may be described as "pockets," it will be open to the cultivator, if he chooses to do so, to place a differently compounded soil in each compartment or pocket, to suit the most exacting requirements of various plants. He might fill the various spaces so as to have, for instance, heavy clay soil in one, light loam in another, peat in a third, sandy soil in a fourth, limestone soil in yet another, and rich leaf-mould in still another. But this would be taking an infinite amount of trouble with very little object.

What may be described as all-round useful soil will suffice probably for the requirements of most cultivators, who do not want to make a toil of their pleasant recreation ; and upon such a soil as we will suggest a vast number of plants will live and thrive and be a " joy," practically, for ever.

Comparatively few plants require a heavy clay soil, but the majority of plants rejoice in a light porous soil, and all require leaf-mould, or decayed vegetable matter, for that contains their vital food. Hence a combination, in about equal proportions, of rich loam, leaf-mould, peat, and sand will constitute a soil that will suit the requirements of hundreds of different species. Indeed, the common soil of almost any garden will enable scores of most interesting plants to live and thrive. But after a time it must be understood that the rich nutritive elements of the soil will be absorbed, or exhausted, by the roots, and then more leaf-mould should be spread upon all the earthy surfaces. The air contains gases which will be communicated to the soil, and rain provides other contributions ; and therefore, so to speak, the merely automatic action of the elements will be continually replenishing what has been withdrawn in order to build up the beautiful fabrics of plant structure.

For those who may take delight in the physiology of plants it will be open to provide the multifarious elemental substances which may suit what may be called the idiosyncrasies of individual species ; but this little volume has been written, as it is stated in our preface, for those who want to get a maximum of instruction and amusement, with a minimum of trouble.

We by no means dissuade our readers from the study of what may be called the chemistry of soils. It will prove a most interesting subject for all who go deeply into it ; but it is not necessary any more than it is necessary for the pedestrian who is longing to take a walk to delay the delightful exercise until he has mastered the anatomy of the foot ; for the hungry man to avoid eating until he has made himself conversant with the science of digestion ; or for the thirsty man to refrain from drinking until he is well up in the chemical constituents of liquids.

VI

FORMATION

THIS is a most vitally important chapter, because it is absolutely necessary for the rockery-maker to grasp " first principles," or his endeavour to obtain amusement and delight from the rocky parts of his garden will end in woeful disappointment. Hundreds of plants will take care of themselves in almost any kind of soil, provided that soil is kept moist ; but unless rockery is properly made they will be open to the constant risk of perishing from drought.

The author has seen a good many rockeries, but he is bound to assert that not one in ten is properly made. It cannot even be conceded that the defective rockeries are ornamental when they are not useful. Nature's arrangement is the most picturesque and the most beautiful method, as well as the most useful, and yet Nature is not followed in nine out of ten cases.

In the evolution of a natural rockery already alluded to, gravitation usually causes the largest blocks of stone to descend to the lowest positions ; for even if some small fragments were first in getting to the ground they could not bear up under the enormous weight of superposed masses, and the latter would, therefore, oftentimes find their way underneath the others. Where volcanic agency has formed a hill, and subsequent explosions have caused huge fragments of rock to be flung out from its summit, the largest blocks may not necessarily roll down into the lower positions, but may be arrested midway by some small obstructions, or, colliding against each other, may roll and settle into positions that could not be previously anticipated.

A probable explanation of the discovery, amidst the stones of a natural rockery, of great blocks of a kind different from that of the local or adjacent strata is that they were frozen, during the glacial age, on to huge icebergs which subsequently floated them longer or shorter distances from the places where they originally lay; and then, during later thaws, dropped them into the positions they now occupy.

But when the waters had receded, and what was primeval lake or sea became dry land, then began the process attending the production of surface soil, the filling up with that soil of every hollow space between the rocky masses, and the appearance, in due course, of growing grass, moss, fern, shrub, or tree.

For interesting object lessons of a great natural rockery, let us take a little series of studies; and we will select the spots for illustration from the wild and beautiful region of Dartmoor. The series were all photographed by us from one hill-side. No. 1 (page 27) shows a grassy bridle-path, by the margin of which huge masses of rock are piled on either hand. The path is seen to be ascending ; the stony surfaces are clothed with moss and lichen, interspersed with little sprays of ivy. For many hundreds of years the great rocks have lain in their present

1. A grassy bridle-path through huge masses of rock (page 26).

position. The mind will easily go back to a time when all was arid and bare, and the age of vegetation had not arrived, and picture a scene of desolation. No. 2 (page 29) will give a little scene of great variety and beauty. The masses of rocks are various in size and the hollows between have been filled, not only with grass and other soft herbaceous covering, and with bracken, whose dead fronds, for it is winter, nestle in the interstices, but with bramble and gorse. As with the others so with these, ivy trails upon the rocky surface and moss and lichen are interspersed.

A rocky scene of great beauty is exhibited in our picture No. 3 (page 29), where the great stony masses are seen to have been flung across each other in wild and weird confusion. The bare forms of young trees are seen springing in places from amidst the recumbent rocky masses, and these indicate a depth of soil which it has taken a long period to produce. Moss, lichen, and ivy contrast with the patches disclosed here and there of grim, grey rock ; whilst, in the foreground of our little scene, the picturesque dead fronds of brake are mementoes and reminders of the graceful feathery forms that, but a few months before, were waving in the summer breeze.

Again the scene changes, as we near the

2. The masses of rock are various in size (page 27).

3. Great stony masses are seen to have been flung against each other (page 28).

hill-top, and blue sky begins to peep above the crests of the higher rocks depicted in No. 4 (page 31). One small but solitary mass lies in the nearer foreground, whilst above and around are masses of varying shapes and sizes in the deep, moist hollows between which young trees, now bare of leaves, spring up. The picture, as shown in our scene, does not disclose the rich brown fronds of dead bracken, which, when alive in summer, rise above the picturesque boulders of grey, ivy-mantled rock.

The slightest movement of the tourist upon such a rocky hill-side as the one we are describing produces a marked and interesting change in the perspective of the scenes and in the general and particular aspect ; and every, even the most minute, change in Nature is absorbingly interesting. How different, for instance, is our picture No. 5 from the preceding one, although the little " bit " of rock scenery was taken only a few yards from the one shown in No. 4. Huge rock boulders are scattered upon the hill-top. Trees are growing out of nearly every moist

4. Above and around are rocky masses of varying shape (page 30).

5. Trees are growing out of nearly every moist, rocky hollow (page 30).

hollow. Where there are no trees the brown fronds of last year's verdant bracken are suggestive of the green life which will spring up directly the softening influence of the succeeding vernal season has permeated the moist rocks, and every individual rocky mass is a study of beauty, in trailing ivy and miniature, infinitesimal, microscopic forests, so to speak, of moss and lichen.

And when we come to our little picture numbered 6 (page 33), what a change of aspect is again revealed! We have now reached the top of the moorland hill-side. To the left is a prospect of moorland beyond our standpoint; above is the delightful blueness of the vault of heaven. The almost central rocky mass is overspread by a green shroud of ivy in tree form that has risen and almost covered the whole of the rocky top. On the right the ramification of a deciduous tree is outlined against the sky. Smaller fragments of rock are scattered about the foreground of the little picture, and in this foreground a cluster of bracken fronds attests the verdant beauty which anon will be crowded into the hollow spaces.

One more picture, No. 7 (page 35), taken from the other side of our rocky eminences, will disclose yet another change in the natural

6. We have now reached the top of the moorland hill-side (page 32).

grouping. Upon three giant masses of stone are superposed other huge blocks. Bramble and bracken fill the immediate foreground, and in the shady crevices of the rocks grow plants which find refreshment and vitality in their cool and moist positions. Here, as elsewhere, the stony surfaces, erstwhile bleak and bare, are crowded by green growths of ivy, moss, and lichen.

The method to be adopted in a garden for the formation of a rockery that shall be as nearly as possible an imitation of a natural one will depend on the character of the available ground. Should the space be undulated and present a more or less steep slope upwards or downwards, to a wall, hedge, or other bounding fence, the task of construction will be somewhat easier, because the slope will constitute an embankment, the earth of which will save the necessity of filling up the body, so to speak, of the work. If a slope of ground descending to a boundary wall be selected for forming a rockery, then a path should be made alongside the wall, so that the rockery could be properly seen and admired by any one standing with his back to the wall. If the ground slopes up to a wall, the path should be on the other side, and the rockwork carried right up to the wall. In either case the first thing to do is to remove grass or anything else growing on the ground and to dig over the entire surface ;

7. Upon three giant masses of stone are superposed other large blocks (page 33).

then to place a row of the largest blocks of stone along the bottom of the slope. These should be placed close together in as irregular and picturesque a manner as possible, using a heavy wooden mallet to knock them as firmly against each other as possible. To test this firmness take hold of the last block with the fingers and thumb of the left hand to see that it is firmly wedged and does not oscillate or otherwise move, and then proceed in the same manner until the first row has been laid down; but as to this first row something has here to be said.

Illustration No. 8 (page 37) is a photograph of one side of a rockery built under an arbutus tree, just inside the entrance to a garden. A path runs up from the gate along the wall shown, and, of course, by the gate, that side of the rockery goes down to the path. On the side shown the largest stones are properly used for the bottom row, but the mistake made by the builder is in standing the longest stones on end, so to speak, instead of laying them on the ground along their greatest length; and the stones are not wedged together as tightly and firmly as they should be. But the actual construction affords an apt illustration of several bad points. As the rockery is erected upon a gravelled path a slight trench, say an inch or two inches deep, should have been made in which to lay the bottom row of big stones. It will be clear to

8. Garden rockery, illustrating some bad points of construction (page 36).

the reader that this trench would catch and retain all water—whether from rain or a watering-pot—falling on, and percolating through, the uppeı stages. It is obvious, too, that otherwise a heavy downpour of rain would wash out on to the path between the stones the earth of the rockery; and it is clear also that if, instead of being placed on end, on the level of the gravelled path, the stones had been placed down lengthwise, and arranged to lie in the shallow trench, it would have been better. Then, instead of the small stones shown in No. 8 as forming the next (upper) row, the next largest boulders forming the third row should have been placed on their sides in the terrace above, each stone in this second (upper) terrace being placed across two stones in the lowermost one, and sunk in the earth of the rockery so that the bottoms of the second row of stones should be put about an inch below the tops of the lowermost row. All water and earth would thus be banked in and prevented from coming through the spaces between the stones.

Moreover, the earth in every "pocket" should be levelled backwards and slightly downwards, and then all surplus water, instead of falling or rolling off like the rain down an umbrella, would be thrown back into the rockery. With regard to this last-mentioned point, we are aware that certain "expert" writers recommend that the slopes of the earthy terraces should be forward, that is to say outwards, on the ground that the

9. A properly constructed one-tier rockery.

sloping inwards might cause the body of earth to become sodden at times. But we strongly hold to the contrary opinion, as far more mischief is likely to occur from drought than from occasional excess of moisture.

Proper construction is much better shown

in the rockery illustrated in No. 9 (page 39), but this is practically little more than a one-tier structure. The outer stones in this oval rockery, put up on a gravelled path, are properly laid down lengthwise and slightly sunk in the gravel of the pathway; but as they are covered by a mossy growth the relative positions of the lower and upper stones cannot be very clearly noted. The crown of the rockery is practically an open bed in which big evergreen and bushy shrubs have been planted. If this rockery had been made, in its lower row, like that of No. 8, heavy rain, or even the ordinary watering with a pot or hose, would wash out the earth and stain and disfigure the gravelled path.

A much better formation is shown in illustration No. 10 (page 41), where a bank to the left of the stone steps leading up to a higher terrace of the garden is covered by very picturesque blocks of limestone. Points of criticism may, however, be suggested—taking the first four blocks in the lowermost row, counting from the bottom of the stone steps to the left. The first block next and to the left of the steps should have been put down lengthwise instead of being stood on end, and so should the second block next to it. The third and fourth stones are placed down

10. A picturesque limestone rockery adjoining garden steps.

correctly, but the fifth should have been put down lengthwise instead of on end. The stone on the second and upper tier, instead of being wedged into the depression between the third and fourth of the lowermost row, should have been put down lengthwise across the division between those two stones, and so on, upwards, the same plan should have been adopted.

Reverting to the question of forming a rockery on a sloping bank, now that explanation has been made of preliminary principles of arrangement, it should be carefully noted that so soon as the lowermost row of stones has been correctly laid lengthwise along the bottom of the slope, the part of the bank level with the top of the stones should be dug back about a foot, making it slightly slope inwards, and then the second row of stones should be laid, each stone tightly wedged with the help of the wooden mallet, across each two of the stones below. They should be well hammered into the terrace of earth, so that no space be left between the bottoms of the upper row and the tops of the lower ones, beyond the pockets of earth shown in No. 10 (page 41). The bank above the second row of stones should then be dug back in the same manner as advised for the first terrace, and the third row of stones placed along on the same plan as for the second; and so on right to the highest point to which it is desired to carry the rockwork. When finished every stone above should lean tightly against every stone below, and if further strengthening and consolidation are required, Portland cement can be used to fill into little crevices between the stones in small places or pockets, the filling up of which will not materially interfere with the total amount of "pocket" space required for planting. If this cementing be carefully done the whole rockery will be one solid mass of rockwork, "honeycombed," so to speak, by the plant openings. This consolidation will greatly assist in keeping the whole surface moist, even during droughts.

Before applying the Portland cement the surfaces of stone against which the cement is to be placed should be washed clean, so as to be free from earth or moss or lichen. It is often necessary, in fact, to scrape the surface to enable the cement to adhere well.

In making the cement, dry sharp sand—

such as that which can be obtained from a river bottom—should be well mixed into it whilst dry, in the proportion of equal parts of sand and pure Portland cement ; or one part of cement and two parts of sand will make a fairly good cement and will be less costly. For the mixing a trowel should be used and the mixing continued until the entire blend is one uniform colour. Water should then be added and stirred in until a sort of thick paste is made, and then it should be applied quickly with a trowel to the pieces of rock it is intended to hold together. Cementing should not be done during frosty weather. A very little practice will soon make the rockery builder expert at the work.

When a rockery has to be made on level ground, and round, oval, or irregular in shape, standing by itself in a gravel path or grass lawn, after the first row of stones has been placed around the space allotted to the rockery, earth must be filled in to the level of the tops of the lowermost row of rocks and well rammed down to prevent subsidence later on. Then the second row of stones should be put round and earth again filled in to the tops of the second row, and thus again rammed down ; and so on right to the top.

If larger spaces be required than would be left by the stones being rammed close together, a stone here and there could be omitted ; but it is much better to make these larger spaces by using bigger blocks of stone for the upper terraces, and these, wedged across the lower ones, would make larger "pockets," or compartments.

A rockery can easily be formed in the angle made by the meeting of walls. The distance out from the wall—allowed for the rockery—should be measured, and a line of stones, marking the outer limit, should be placed from wall to wall. Earth should then be rammed in to the tops of the outer row. A further line should be placed inside the first one, the earth again filled in and rammed down to the level of the second row of stones ; and the process thus carried on until the whole of the enclosed space is filled in with rockery. The work can be stopped at any moment should a larger space, or spaces, be required for planting at the top of the rockery; but every tier of earth should be carefully sloped inwards and backwards, so as to ensure that all water, whether from rain, watering-pot, or hose, shall be absorbed into the body of the construction.

VII

FERN ROCKERY

FERNS are naturally rock-growing plants, and although often found thriving away from rocks, they thrive best when, with rich soil of leaf-mould underneath, the surface of the ground is covered by large or small masses of stone. The secret of this exceptional growth lies in the greater degree of moisture induced when a stony covering prevents evaporation.

One or two illustrations of the appearance of the flowerless plants on rockery are all that can be given within the limits of this little volume. It is better to show the plants as photographed growing singly than attempt to show them growing in the mass, for thus there would be confusion as to their identity.

Later on in the chapter figures will be given

of a number of British ferns grouped in plates from the illustrations in the author's "Fern Paradise"; and these will be included for purposes of identification.

Engraving No. 11 (page 49) is one that gives what the French would call a *coup d'œil* of a rockery constructed some years ago by the author in his garden at Richmond. It is extremely difficult to represent in one photograph what this rockery looked like, because the intensity of light was so much greater in parts of it than in other parts that an equally-balanced picture could not be obtained. Those of our readers who understand photography will know that sufficient exposure for the shadows of the rockery—and this rockery was chiefly in perpetual shadow—would "over-expose" what are known as the "high lights" or the sunny parts; but some verbal explanation accompanying the photograph will give an idea of what a visitor one day described as "a dream of beauty."

The author made every bit of this rockery with his own hands. Instead of first making

11. Our own rockery, with a series of miniature lakes and waterfalls descending sixteen feet into the ground (page 48).

E

the big excavation that would have been necessary if the work had been commenced at the bottom—for the rockery was carried down sixteen feet into the ground—the reverse of that proceeding was adopted.

Rocks were laid around in a large circle, or rather in the form of a parallelogram, on the surface of the ground and these were undermined, in sets of two at a time, and rocks wedged under these. By undermining rather less than half of each two rocks on the top or first row, the latter were prevented from falling in. Then a further rock was wedged under the two rather less than half-undermined upper rocks, and this process was extended round the parallelogram until a second continuous row had been made; and so on, downwards, each additional under row being slanted inwards. As each row was completed the whole was cemented, and each under row was also in due course cemented in the same way, and also cemented to the row above. When about half-way towards the required depth one of the four sides was left as a sort of slanting terrace, and the deepening on that side continued downwards less steeply, and in the centre of this gradual descent a series of miniature lakes or basins was made as shown in the picture, each basin being lower than the preceding one. Water at high pressure being obtainable and supplied especially for garden watering, was admitted at the highest point and from that point it fell into the first miniature lake. As it overflowed that one it fell at its lower end into the one below. To prevent its flowing out on any other side but the lower one the three other sides were built above the level of the latter, and to enable small fish to be kept in the little lakes and prevented from swimming out with the outflow of water, pieces of perforated zinc were cemented across, the upper edges of which were level with the other three sides of each little basin. On each side of the central series of miniature lakes and waterfalls level terraces of earth were left for planting ferns, primroses, wild violets, ivy, brambles, and other wildings, and all the rocky crevices were similarly filled. Across the terraces flanking the miniature lakes large blocks of stone were put at irregular intervals, and each line or ridge of stone—piece being tightly hammered against piece—made to extend from the raised sides of the little basins to the almost perpendicular sides of the rockery. These ridges were placed to prevent the earth of the terraces from being washed down into the bottom of the rockery during the torrential rains that sometimes occur even in this country.

It is rather difficult to give a verbal description, that shall be perfectly clear to the reader, of this rather unique construction; but its form and plan will perhaps be understood by the aid of the engraving No. 11. It was about fifty feet long by twenty feet broad at its widest (upper part). In summer, when the ferns in it—Hartstongues, buckler ferns, shield ferns, polypodies, spleenworts, osmundas, and lady ferns—were in their full splendour, and the water was musically tumbling down over the edges of the lakes in little cascades, finally dropping from the lowermost basin, like an infinitesimal "Niagara," into the depths of the rockery, the aspect of the whole was exceedingly beautiful. The author's intention was to imitate a Devonshire gully, or rocky hill-side lane down which a stream rushes from the heights above; and the highest compliment that was paid to his success was in the building—in his imitation—during two successive years, by blackbirds, of nests in which young families were reared. The nests were placed upon a broad, rocky ridge, forming a foundation for the building materials, and sheltered by overarching sprays of bramble. The object of carrying the rockwork down into the ground not quite perpendicularly, but with a very steep slant inwards, was to afford protection for the more delicate plants against frost. For this purpose the sides must not be too far apart, because it is the radiation of warmth from them that creates a sort of underground temperature higher than that in the open garden.

Illustration No. 12 (page 55) was photographed by the author from a fern as it grew in full beauty on a little bit of rockwork—hidden by the spreading fronds—against a clump of shrubbery forming its dark background. It represents the Lady fern (*Athyrium filix-fœmina*), which is probably the most graceful and beautiful of all our native ferns. Any plant whose parts, leaves or fronds, spread like this one is a difficult subject for the ordinary camera, because whilst the parts nearest the latter are got into focus the more distant parts, in what may be called a "near view," will be rather out of focus. An object such as a straight wall, or an engraving pinned against a vertical board, will "photograph" well, all parts of it, when equidistant from the lens, being equally sharp in the resulting copy. No. 13 (page 55) gives another pretty view of the same plant, taken from another point and showing the gravelled path leading through the shrubbery. In engraving No. 17, Fig. 3 (page 61) a representation of a pressed frond of the Lady fern

12. The Lady Fern (*Athyrium filix-fœmina*).

13. Another view of the Lady Fern.

will be shown ; but whilst that will be more useful for the purpose of identifying the frond of *Athyrium filix-fœmina* Nos. 12 and 13 will give a much better idea of the plant as a whole in its exquisite symmetry of form. The Lady fern is an admirable subject for the fern rockery, but except where the latter is very large and there is ample space in each "compartment" for the full display of its spreading fronds, the lowermost tier of the rockery is the best for it, because there is usually to be found the greatest amount of shade and moisture.

Next to the Lady fern in gracefulness and beauty, and superior to it in hardy adaptation for the garden rockery, is the Soft prickly Shield fern (*Polystichum angulare*), which is practically evergreen, especially in sheltered places. It will really grow anywhere and in any soil ; but it best loves a moist, shady position and plenty of leaf-mould. The engraving No. 14 (page 57) shows how much grace and beauty it will lend to a dark corner when peeping out of a little bit of rockery.

14. Soft Prickly Shield Fern (*Polystichum angulare*).

15. Fern rockery against house wall.
Growing Hartstongues and Soft Prickly Shield Ferns.

The transformation from the aridness and ugliness of a bare house wall when lightened by a little bit of rockery containing Harts-tongues on the top, and Soft prickly Shield ferns in the lower " pockets," is exemplified by No. 15 (page 57). What exquisite grace is spread over, so to speak, the bare stones by these two or three ferns !

No. 16 (page 59) does not, perhaps, make a very striking picture ; but the reality is much more striking than the photograph. It represents a young Royal fern (*Osmunda regalis*) growing in a nook of the big rockery —close to one of the miniature lakes—shown in engraving No. 11 (page 49). The feature of interest in this picture is in the fertile fronds of *Osmunda regalis ;* the way in which the spore cases are clustered round them gives them somewhat the appearance of flowering spikes. Hence one of the names—" Flowering fern "—given to *Osmunda regalis.* If the reader will apply a magnifying glass to these fertile fronds he will see in them some interesting detail.

16. Royal Fern (*Osmunda regalis*).
Showing barren and fertile fronds.

And now for a very brief reference to the greater or less adaptability, for rockery, of the British ferns figured in the succeeding five plates—Nos. 17, 18, 19, 20, and 21—borrowed from "The Fern Paradise." As already premised, all ferns are rock-loving plants, that is to say, they are to be found associated more or less with rock scenery, and they all appreciate the greater moisture obtainable by their roots when the presence of rocks on the surface of the ground prevents evaporation of moisture. It may also be premised that, as all the ferns mentioned are hardy enough to grow out of doors in the British Islands—although the range of some of them is confined to particular parts of those Islands, there is no reason whatever why they should not be successfully grown upon open garden rockery if the latter imitates the conditions under which the ferns grow wild, and if the ferns are planted on garden rockery in the same districts in which the ferns are, or have been, found growing wild.

To begin, then, with No. 17 and Fig. 1,

17. Group of British Ferns.

1 Bracken (*Pteris aquilina*).
2. Hartstongue (*Scolopendrium vulgare*).
3. Lady Fern (*Athyrium filix-fœmina*).
4 Hard Fern (*Blechnum spicant*).
5. Royal Fern (*Osmunda regalis*).
6. True Maidenhair (*Adiantum capillus-veneris*).
7. Parsley Fern (*Allosorus crispus*).
8. Bristle Fern (*Trichomanes radicans*).
9. Moonwort (*Botrychium lunaria*).
10. Adderstongue (*Ophioglossum vulgatum*).
11 Little Adderstongue (*Ophioglossum lusitanicum*).

the Bracken (*Pteris aquilina*)—deciduous—grows almost everywhere throughout the British Islands, often covering large tracts of ground, especially in mountain, moorland, and forestal regions. On rockery it will require a big "compartment," and to successfully transplant it, it is best to secure small plants, growing on shallow, rocky soil, so that a patch of it may be taken up without disturbing the *rhizomas*, or underground horizontally creeping rootstocks. A frond with a little black substance at foot looking like a root will not suffice.

The Hartstongue (*Scolopendium vulgare*)—evergreen—Fig. 2, is extremely plentiful and is almost as widely distributed in these Islands, from the sea-level to six hundred feet above it, as the Bracken. It can be transplanted at any time and of any size, and fitted into any little "pocket," or "compartment," of garden rockery that will easily take it; but allowance must be made for its growing. It is a most delightful fern for rockery.

The Lady fern (*Athyrium filix-fœmina*)—deciduous—Fig. 3, is aptly described in the pretty lines :—

Not by burn, in wood, or dale,
Grows anything so fair
As the plumy crests of emerald pale
That wave in the wind or sough in the gale
Of the Lady Fern, when the sunbeams turn
To gold her delicate hair.

And the following lines will also suggest, perhaps better than anything else, how to treat, on rockery, this exquisite member of the fern family :—

Where the copsewood is the greenest,
Where the fountains glisten sheenest,
Where the morning dew lies longest,
There the Lady Fern grows strongest.

Its beautiful fronds must have plenty of room to spread, and it must have, at all times, an abundance of water for its roots. Standing quite alone, as is shown, for instance, in engravings Nos. 12 and 13 (page 55), it adds indescribable grace to its position. The shadiest as well as the moistest parts of rockery are the best suited for this really beautiful plant. The Lady fern is also pretty widely distributed throughout the British Islands, from sea-level to three thousand feet above it, and so may be grown in any garden anywhere.

Often found in company with it, in similarly moist and shady positions, and almost as widely distributed as the Lady fern, is the Hard fern (*Blechnum spicant*), Fig. 4. On rockery it is best placed at the very bottom, or on the ground tier. It is evergreen.

The Royal fern (*Osmunda regalis*), Fig. 5—deciduous—is naturally a large-growing species and it thrives best in the most moist and shady positions, which cannot be too wet—as, for instance, adjoining the spray of a fountain or close to a running stream—provided the position is well drained, that is to say, not waterlogged.

The True Maidenhair (*Adiantum capillus-veneris*) is ordinarily grown only—that is to say, this native British species—in cool greenhouses ; but, although we have never seen it placed on outdoor rockery, it is quite possible it would grow in a garden on rockery—if the position were the same—close to or near the sea, and exposed to sea air, on limestone rock and in the same districts in this country as this beautiful fern is found growing wild in. It has been found growing wild on the coast of North Devon and also in the same county, near Brixham ; on the Cheddar Cliffs in Somersetshire ; on rocks in parts of Wales ; on rocks in Kincardineshire ; on and near the west and other coasts of Ireland ; in the Isle of Man, and in Jersey and Guernsey. As it will grow well in a greenhouse anywhere, it may be assumed that wherever it can be kept with a greenhouse temperature and general "conditions," that is to say, with a continuously moist atmosphere, in leaf-mould and between pieces of limestone rock, wedged in so that its rootlets can easily penetrate the seams of rock and its *rhizomas* be kept moist and enabled to creep on the damp, porous, rocky surface, it would grow and even thrive.

The Parsley fern (*Allosorus crispus*), Fig. 7 —deciduous—commonly called the Mountain

Parsley fern, is confined in its range to the north of England, North Wales, and Scotland, and a few parts of Ireland; but always in mountainous regions is it found thriving best. If planted elsewhere it will grow for a time, but gradually dwindle. Hence on garden rockery in its native districts, if grown in the higher and drier parts of such rockery, and not kept too moist, and if planted in what may be called mountain soil, peat, leaf-mould, and sand, it should do well.

Trichomanes radicans (the Bristle fern), Fig. 8—evergreen—was said to have once been found growing wild in Yorkshire, and also in Wales. Its favourite wild habitats are in the south of Ireland, chiefly in the county of Cork; but a perpetually moist atmosphere and an atmosphere heavily charged with moisture (as, for instance, close to a waterfall) is absolutely essential to the successful growth of this exquisitely beautiful fern; and as it is almost impossible, on any open rockery unless close to a waterfall, to maintain these conditions, the only way to extemporise them is to sink a compartment of such rockery about three feet, making practically a hole three feet deep—to put at the bottom of this hole some lumps of free-stone, filled in with peat, leaf-mould, and sand, to plant the *rhizomas* of the Bristle fern amongst the lumps of stone and then to cover the hole (after well watering the fern) with a piece of glass. The particular compartment of rockery just described would have to be accessible, so that the glass cover could be lifted to enable the fern to be admired.

The Moonwort (*Botrychium lunaria*), Fig. 9, the Adderstongue (*Ophioglossum vulgatum*), Fig. 10, and the Little Adderstongue (*Ophio-glossum lusitanicum*), Fig. 11, are three interesting, deciduous little ferns, rather widely distributed throughout the kingdom and growing in more or less damp meadows amongst grass, the presence of which, curiously enough, seems essential to their well-being. They form interesting subjects for the more open parts of rockery; but, to ensure successful transplantation, they should be removed from their wild habitats embedded in little "hummocks" of the grass they are found growing in.

No more hardy, desirable, and in all ways delightful ferns can be found for the garden rockery than the very beautiful and evergreen Shield ferns, figured in illustration No. 18 (page 69)—the Hard prickly Shield fern (*Polystichum aculeatum*), Fig. 1, the Soft prickly Shield fern (*Polystichum angulare*), Fig. 2, and the Holly fern (*Polystichum lonchitis*), Fig. 3. The two first-named have a pretty wide distribution, but the Holly fern is much more rare. The Soft prickly Shield fern is the most abundant, except in Scotland, and it is wonderfully well adapted for growing in the darkest and shadiest corners. With care and attention it will attain a large size, with fronds three or four feet long, under cultivation. Plants of all sizes of *P. angulare* can be obtained from hedge-banks in fern country, to suit little "pockets" in the rockery, and sometimes a small aperture will suffice for the crown and rootlets when a

18. The Shield Ferns.

1. Hard Prickly Shield Fern (*Polystichum aculeatum*).
2. Soft Prickly Shield Fern (*Polystichum angulare*).
3. Holly Fern (*Polystichum lonchitis*).

small specimen has grown in size; but the fronds will spread out, making a very graceful and beautiful display. It is important, however, to remember in first planting to allow some room for it to enlarge and spread, as, by thus anticipating its requirements, some trouble in transplantation, later on, will be saved.

What are called the Buckler ferns—six in number—are a most interesting group for the garden rockery. Perhaps the hardiest, the most widely distributed, and, therefore, the best-known of these is the Common Buckler fern, or "Male fern," as it is generally called—the term "Male fern" being only applied to it because of its robust appearance as distinguished from the delicate-looking, but unrelated, "Lady fern." The Common Buckler fern—*Lastrea filix-mas*—is sub-evergreen, and it will grow well in the general rockery soil already described. Plate 19, Fig. 1 (page 71), shows the form of the frond. It may be put into a sunny position if its roots be kept well watered, but acquires its finest

19. The Buckler Ferns.

1. Male (or Common Buckler) Fern (*Lastrea filix-mas*).
2. Broad Buckler Fern (*Lastrea dilatata*).
3. Hay-scented Buckler Fern (*Lastrea recurva*).
4. Prickly-toothed Buckler Fern (*Lastrea spinulosa*).
5. Mountain Buckler Fern (*Lastrea montana*)
6. Marsh Buckler Fern (*Lastrea thelypteris*).

form in the shade. It is so hardy that, practically, it will grow almost anywhere. The Broad Buckler fern (*Lastrea dilatata*), Fig. 2, is an extremely handsome species, very widely distributed throughout the kingdom, and extremely hardy. It is sub-evergreen and will grow well and acquire a large size on the garden rockery. A very beautiful fern is *Lastrea recurva*, a sub-evergreen, hay-scented species—its botanical or specific name arising from the fact that whilst, in general form, much like the Broad Buckler fern, it is distinguished from the last-named by having the lobes of its pinnules recurved or slightly convex on the under side instead of concave, as in *Lastrea dilatata*. It is not nearly so widely distributed as the other *Lastreas*, but is a most interesting species, and is especially noticeable on account of the perfume of the fronds—especially when pressed by the fingers. Fig. 4, the Prickly-toothed Buckler fern (*Lastrea spinulosa*), is another interesting member of the group. It rejoices when growing wild in the damp, mossy, shady parts of woods, where, in fact, the ground is rather boggy; and to ensure its success on the garden rockery its natural proclivities should, so far as is possible, be borne in mind. It is more widely distributed than *Lastrea recurva*. Its, so to speak, aromatic peculiarities are shared by the Mountain Buckler fern (*Lastrea montana*), Fig. 5, very often called the lemon-scented fern. It is deciduous, but during spring and summer grows in great abundance in the mountainous and high moorland regions it prefers; and although it is inclined to dwindle in size when transplanted to gardens in lower regions, it will thrive well when its garden conditions are assimilated to its wild ones. Proximity to water is a position that this very beautiful fern loves. It will be noticed from our engraving that it is mainly distinguishable from the Male fern, which in other respects it resembles, by the rapid shortening of the *pinnæ* of the frond towards the bottom of the stipes, or leafy stem of the frond. The last of the Buckler group to mention is a very exacting species—the Marsh Buckler fern (*Lastrea thelypteris*), Fig. 6, which bears a rather strong resemblance both to the Male fern and the Mountain Buckler fern; but its fronds are not scented and its general appearance is very fragile. It loves the very deepest shade and requires so much moisture that nothing but a quite boggy soil would suit it. As its common name implies, it grows in absolutely marshy positions—positions, in fact, which, in a wood, are dangerously boggy. In the most complete shade, where its delicate *rhizomas* can creep along on the surface of what is practically almost liquid peat or leaf soil, it throws up its delicate fronds in profusion and with an elegant grace which is very striking. For it to succeed, therefore, on rockery, a position must be reserved for it in a large compartment, where the natural conditions just described can be extemporised.

Another most interesting little group of ferns, admirably adapted for the garden rockery, bears the descriptive name of the

Polypodies, or the many-footed ferns, so called because their *rhizomas*, or creeping, semi-underground root-stocks, run in different forking directions, like feet—many feet; and as they run they throw out below numerous roots that penetrate the leafy soil or soft rock over which they crawl, and throw up, above, miniature forests of pretty fronds, the various shapes of which—in our native group—are shown at a glance in the little plate reproduced from "The Fern Paradise" and figuring here as engraving No. 20 (page 77). The first to be noticed is Fig. 1, the Common Polypody (*Polypodium vulgare*), evergreen, common only in the sense of being plentiful. Almost everywhere throughout the British Islands this delightful plant is to be found—in hedge-banks, crowding around old tree stumps, and revelling in accumulations of leaf-mould; on old walls, and sometimes on nearly new ones, on rocks and in the hollow "nooks" filled with leaf-mould and furnished by tree forks in old forests and copses and other woods. It is an excellent fern for the upper terraces of garden rockery, especially where it can get soft masses of stone on which to fasten its "many feet." Fig. 2 is the Mountain Polypody (*Polypodium phegopteris*), a deciduous species, much more delicate than its "common" relative, and less widely distributed. It is to be found chiefly, as its specific name indicates, in mountainous regions and more especially in damp woods and in the vicinity of mountain streams. The cultivator should learn in what regions it grows wild, and there he will have no difficulty in getting it to like his garden rockery. The Three-branched Polypody (*Polypodium dryopteris*), Fig. 3, deciduous also, is a delicately beautiful little fern, earning its specific common name as a glance at its frond will show. It occurs also in mountainous woods, but it loves a drier position than does *P. phegopteris*. Where it grows wild, and indeed elsewhere, when shade and leaf-mould and a moist atmosphere are available, it will thrive on garden rockery. Its distribution is very much the same as that of the

20. The Polypodies.

1. Common Polypody (*Polypodium vulgare*).
2. Mountain Polypody (*Polypodium phegopteris*).
3. Three-branched Polypody (*Polypodium dryopteris*).
4. Limestone Polypody (*Polypodium calcareum*).
5. Alpine Polypody (*Polypodium alpestre*).

last-named ; but the limits of the Limestone Polypody (*Polypodium calcareum*), Fig. 4—deciduous—are defined by the limits of limestone rocks on which it grows. It is hardier and larger in size than either *P. phegopteris* or *P. dryopteris*, but will favour rockery where it can creep upon masses of limestone.

The Alpine Polypody (*Polypodium alpestre*), Fig. 5—deciduous—is a very beautiful fern, very much in its general appearance like the Lady fern, and quite adaptable for growth on well-drained, shady rockery ; but it is much more rare—as it has only been found wild in Scotland—than either of its four relations just described.

There could not be a more delightful little group of rockery plants than the British evergreen spleenworts. Some of them are very plentiful and widely distributed ; others are more rare ; but all are beautiful. Noticing them in the order in which they are figured in our engraving No. 21 (page 79), we come first to Fig. 1, the Forked Spleenwort. It is a very unpretending little plant, something like

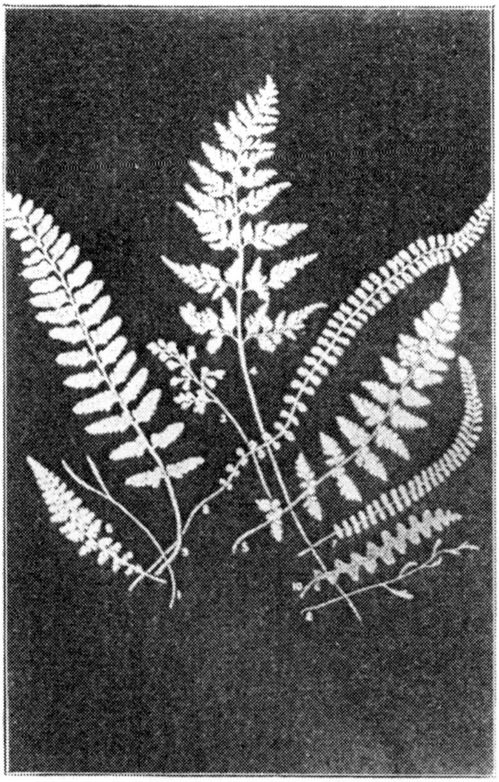

21. The Spleenworts.

1. Forked Spleenwort (*Asplenium septentrionale*).
2. Alternate Spleenwort (*Asplenium germanicum*).
3. Rue-leaved Spleenwort (*Asplenium ruta-muraria*).
4. Black Maidenhair Spleenwort (*Asplenium adiantum-nigrum*).
5. Lanceolate Spleenwort (*Asplenium lanceolatum*).
6. Rock Spleenwort (*Asplenium fontanum*).
7. Green Spleenwort (*Asplenium viride*).
8. Common Maidenhair Spleenwort (*Asplenium trichomanes*).
9. Sea Spleenwort (*Asplenium marinum*).
10. Scaly Spleenwort (*Asplenium ceterach*).

a small tuft of grass ; and yet it is very rare—*Asplenium septentrionale.* It grows in Wales and in one or two English counties ; very sparingly in Scotland, and not at all in Ireland. The would-be cultivator, therefore, who desired to get some specimens at once would have to resort to the fern nurseries. A very stony " habitat " would have to be found for it. The Alternate Spleenwort (*Asplenium germanicum*), Fig. 2, is also rare and its distribution is confined to a few places in England, Wales, and Scotland. It requires, as indeed do all the spleenworts, a well-drained position on the garden rockery—care being taken that no stagnant moisture surrounds it. The Rue-leaved Spleenwort, or Wall Rue (*Asplenium ruta-muraria*), is very much more abundant throughout the kingdom and is frequently seen on old walls along waysides and elsewhere, as well as very abundantly on rocks. The little crannies or cracks that may be found on many lumps of rock would be the best positions in which to place the wiry rootlets of this pretty little fern, with its tiny, fleshy, wedge-shaped pinnules.

Fig. 4, the Black maidenhair Spleenwort (*Asplenium adiantum-nigrum*), is a plentiful and extremely beautiful fern, with dark green, glossy, beautifully-cut pinnules. This occurs abundantly on the crevices of old walls, and in tiny forms on new ones; also in rocky crevices of all kinds. But in rich leaf-mould deposits in old hedge-banks, especially those which are largely constructed of stone, it is found growing to a large size; and in garden rockery in almost any "pocket" in which there is an abundance of leaf-mould, moisture, and shade it will attain large proportions and thrive well. The Lanceolate Spleenwort (*Asplenium lanceolatum*), Fig. 5, favours rocky habitats that are within the influence of the sea. It is very much like the Black maidenhair Spleenwort, but is distinguishable from that by having its lower pinnules contracted in size, as shown in the figure—the frond, widest in the middle, tapering towards each end—thus being lance-shaped, as its name indicates, instead of being triangular in shape owing to the longest pinnules being the bottom pair on the frond, as in the Black maidenhair Spleenwort. The roots of this fern are best placed in narrow crevices of pieces of rock in the garden rockery. Fig. 6, the Rock Spleenwort (*Asplenium fontanum*) is a very elegant little fern, but very rare, occurring wild in a few places only in the middle and north of England, in Wales, in Scotland, and in Ireland, in which country only one habitat has been named. The Green Spleenwort (*Asplenium viride*), Fig. 7, is also confined chiefly to middle and northern parts of England, to Wales, Scotland, and to a few places in Ireland; but it is found in mountainous regions on rocks where there is a trickle of running water. In appearance it is very much like Fig. 8, the Common maidenhair Spleenwort (*Asplenium trichomanes*), a very abundant and widely distributed species, the distinction being that the rachis or stem of the frond in *A. viride* is green, whilst in *A. trichomanes* it is purple. The last-named occurs largely not only on rocks and old walls, but in hedge-banks, where it attains a large size. Fig. 9, the Sea Spleenwort (*Asplenium marinum*), is chiefly found growing on sea cliffs and in sea caves, but will thrive on garden rockery which lies within the influence of the sea, especially if it be planted on pieces of sandstone rock and has the benefit of an ooze of moisture. But the beautiful Scaly Spleenwort (*Asplenium ceterach*), Fig. 10, inhabiting the top parts of old walls and the soft crannies of rock, likes a higher and drier position, free from any drip from plants above it.

Many hardy exotic ferns can also be planted on garden rockwork; but probably our list of native species will suffice for the ordinary cultivator.

VIII

FLOWERING PLANTS

WILD AND OTHERWISE

WHILST in the preceding chapter we have given illustrations of the majority of our native ferns because the species, all told, only run to about forty-five in number —the variations from normal or specific types extending, however, to many hundreds—wild and garden flowers are far too numerous to permit, within our limits, in this little volume, of the inclusion of engravings of even a small proportion, fairly representative of those which are suitable for planting on garden rockery.

But what we shall give is a pretty full list of flowering plants suitable for growing on garden rockery, indicating against each such particulars of height, colour of flower, time of flowering, and other data as may give all the information the cultivator will require. For obtaining all except the species that will be found growing wild the lists of large nurseries should be procured, and a very full and descriptive list can be got from Messrs. Dicksons, the Royal Nurseries, Chester. Here the order of alphabetical arrangement will be that of the botanical name, but against each botanical name the popular or English name will be given; and, to enable this name—a most interesting and important one for the ordinary reader—to be found, the alphabetical arrangement will be given in the index at the end of the volume; so that, on referring there for a familiar name, whether botanical or English, both names can be obtained and put together on turning to the page of the volume, which gives them side by side.

We shall put into this chapter just one little engraving, No. 22 (page 87), to illustrate an idea rather than the plant portrayed. The plant pictured is the familiar wild primrose of the lane, bank, and wood—the progenitor of the small host of its garden descendants that are known to the gardener best under the generic name *Primula*. There is an indefinable charm in associating the primrose "by the river's brim" with rockery; and the same charm will be found to linger, so to speak, around other wild, or garden, flowers associated with rockery. The author "extemporised" this little picture by placing a primrose (immediately it was taken from the ground, with its delicately fresh golden green leaves, in a "clump" of moist earth—in which its fleshy roots were embedded—and its glorious "wreath" of beautiful blossoms, not one of which was dimmed by the touch of decay) into a little surrounding cluster of rock, and then photographing the "vignette," so to speak, of loveliness before its beauty could pale. Let the reader get a clump of primroses in blossom or a similar clump of the lesser celandine, whose strikingly verdant leaves and golden blossoms unfold to appear "before the swallow dares" to "touch the winds of March with beauty."

Now for our stern and practical rockery flowering list.

22. The Common Primrose of the lane, bank, and wood.

Acæna novæ zealandiæ—Acæna—4 inches,

crimson, flowers in July and August ; a pretty trailer with elegant foliage ; fruit crimson. *Acantholimon androsaceum*: also *A. glumaceum* and *A. venustum*—Prickly thrift—4 inches, the first-named with crimson, the two others of the genus *Acantholimon* with pink blossom, 4 inches, flowers from June to September ; useful for the upper or dry and sunny parts of rockery. Important to keep them as dry as possible in winter. The foliage is spiny and forms thick, beautifully green "cushions." The following are species of the genus *Achillea*—Milfoil—*A. herba-rota*, white, flowers in July and August, 3 inches ; *A. huteri*, white, flowers in May and June, 6 inches ; *A. reichardtiana*, white, flowers in May and June, silvery foliage, 1 foot ; *A. rupestris*, white, flowers from June to August, 6 inches ; *A. tomentosa*, yellow, flowers from June to August, 6 inches ; *A. umbellata*, white, flowers from June to September, 6 inches ; *Aciphylla colensoi*—Bayonet grass—white, flowers during July and August, 3 feet. It is a New Zealand plant, having spiny thickset foliage. *Adonis amurensis* and *A. pyrenaica*—Pheasant's eye—have yellow flowers ; the plants are 1 foot in height and have star-shaped blossoms. The first-named flowers in February and March, and *A. pyrenaica* in April and May.

Another species, *A. vernalis*, is also yellow-flowered, blooms in April and May and is 9 inches high. *Æthionema cordifolia*—Æthionema—the botanical is also the popular name—has rose-coloured flowers blossoming during June and July and is 3 inches high. *A. grandiflora*, deep pink, flowers from July to September and is 9 inches high. A sunny position for these on the rockery is desirable. *Ajuga metallica-crispa*—Bugle—has deep blue flowers which appear from May to July, is 6 inches high and likes a damp position. The foliage is dark green and "crinkled." *Alsine arietioides*—Alsine—botanical and common names the same—has green blossoms appearing during June and July and is 3 inches high. *A. rosanii* is the same size and flowers at the same time, but the blossom is pink. *Alyssum alpestre*—Madwort—has yellow flowers appearing during May and June, and is 3 inches high. *A. montanum* is yellow in blossom, flowers at the same time, is 6 inches high, and *A. pyrenaicum* has white blossom that appears from May to July and may be expected to grow to 6 inches in height. *Androsace*—the generic botanical and common names being the same—is a genus of plants having evergreen foliage that frequently is covered by silky hairs, and the species like to be in gritty soil in deep fissures of the rockery. As we shall mention ten of these species we will, for brevity, give the indicating words in the order of colour, time of flowering and size. *A. arachnoidea*, white, May to July, 3 inches ; *A. carnea*, flesh-coloured, May to July, 2 inches ; *A. chamæjasme*, white, April to June, 3 inches ; *A. coronopifolia*, white, June to August, 6 inches ; *A. foliosa*, pink, May to July, 6 inches ; *A. laggerii*, pink, May to July, 3 inches ; *A. languinosa*, pink, July and August, 9 inches. *A. obtusifolia*, white and also rose, May and June, 6 inches ; *A. sar-*

mentosa, rose, July and August, 6 inches ; and *A. vitaliana*, yellow, May and June, 3 inches. It is preferable to plant *A. carnea*, *A. laggerii*, and *A. vitaliana* in a rather shady position. A shady position is also desirable for the following *Anemones*—Wind flower : *A. alpina*, white, flowering from June to August, 1 foot ; *A. alpina-sulphurea*, straw-coloured, July and August, 1 foot ; *A. robinsoniana*, azure, June and July, 1 foot ; and *A. vernalis*, blush-rose, May and June, 6 inches. *Antennaria tomentosa* —Snowplant—pink-flowered, with silvery foliage, June and July, 2 inches, is a very pretty little plant and may be used as an edging. *Anthemis aizoon* is the Chamomile, has white blossom, flowers in July and August, and is 6 inches high. *Antirrhinum asarina*—Snapdragon — is yellow, flowers from June to August, and is 3 inches high. *A. glutinosum* and *A. sempervirens* have white and cream-coloured blooms, and are produced on trailing stems. They flower from May to September, are three inches high, enjoy warm positions, not too damp, and will thrive even in the poorest soil. *Arabis albida*—Wall cress—is a pretty little plant bearing white blossoms, flowering from March to June, and it is 6 inches high. A pink-flowering species, in bloom during May and June and 3 inches high, is *A. aubrietioides.* Grass-like foliage and white flowers are borne by *Arenaria balearica*—the Sandwort—whilst the species *A. purpurascens* is purple-flowered, blooms from June to August and is 3 inches high. *Armeria cephalotes alba*—Thrift—is white and *A. c. rubra* is red, both flower during July and August, and each is 1 foot high. Another species, *A. maritima*, is lilac in colour, flowers in June and July, and is 6 inches high, whilst *A. plantaginea* is pale pink, flowers at the same time and is 1 foot in height. *Arnebia echioides* —Prophet's flower—is yellow with brown spots. It comes from the Caucasus mountains, flowers from April to September, grows to a foot in height, and makes an excellent rockery plant, but requires a well-drained "pocket." A rich golden yellow species is *Arnica montana*, that flowers during May and

June and is 9 inches high. The Starwort is of the genus *Aster*, and the following five species, all six inches in height, are very suitable for garden rockery. All flower from May to July. They are named and of colour of blossom as follows: *A. alpinus*, lilac; *A. alpinus-albus*, white; *A. alpinus himalaicus*, blue; *A. alpinus-roseus*, rose-coloured; and *A. speciosus* is blue. *Astragalus hypoglottis* is the Milk Vetch, has purple blossoms, which appear during June and July, and is 6 inches in height. *Aubretia*—Bridesmaid—is popularly also called Aubretia. Its colour is blush-rose, it blossoms from April to June, and is 3 inches high. *Calandrina umbellata* is commonly called Calandrina; the colour of its blossom is magenta, it flowers from May to September, and sometimes later, and it grows ordinarily 6 inches high. A poor soil and a sunny position will suit it, and to get it well established it is a good plan to put the seeds in crevices in the masses of rock, from which they will then grow well. *Campanula*—Bell flower—has a pretty representative in the species *abietina,* whose flowers are blue and borne on stems 6 inches in height. Others of the genus to be recommended for their smallness—a *desideratum* of importance in that it enables the grower to include a greater variety in a small space—are the following, the colours, flowering time, and height being briefly stated. The soil they prefer is a sandy limestone one, and a sunny position is desirable. *C. allionii,* bluish purple, June to August, 4 inches; *C. carnica,* blue, June to August, 6 inches; *C. carpatica,* pale blue, June to September, 9 inches; *C. fergusonii,* blue, June to September, 1 foot; *C. hendersonii,* blue, June to September, 1 foot; *C. isophylla,* blue, June to September, 9 inches; *C. pulla,* dark purple, June and July, 3 inches; *C. rainerii,* bluish purple, June to August, 6 inches; *C. turbinata,* purple-blue, June and July, 6 inches; and *C. waldsteiniana,* blue, May to July, 3 inches. The familiar Wallflower, *Cheiranthus,* is represented by the following very interesting species, which will thrive well on rockery: *C. allionii,* yellow, May and June,

9 inches; *C. alpinus*, yellow, April to July, 9 inches; *C. dillenii*, bronze-purple, April to June, 9 inches; and *C. marshallii*, orange, May to August, 9 inches. We must not forget the beautiful Lily of the Valley, *Convallaria*, of which we will name five that will adorn any rockery. These are *C. majalis*, white, May and June; *C. majalis flora-plena*, white; *C. marginata*, white, May and June; *C. rosea*, blush-rose, May and June; and *C. striata*, white, May and June. All these five are 9 inches in height. *Cortusa matthiolii*—Bear's ear sanicle—has red blossoms, flowers April to June, is 6 inches high, and *C. pubens* is bright pink, flowers May and June, and is 6 inches in height. *Corydalis* is the Fumitory; and here are five suitable for rockery: *C. lútea*, yellow, June to September, 1 foot; *C. nobilis*, yellow, May to July, 1½ feet; *C. scouleri*, rose, April and May, 1 foot; *C. solida*, pink, March and April, 6 inches; and *C. thalictrifolia*, pale yellow, June and July, 6 inches; *Crucianella stylosa*—Crosswort—a trailing plant, is pale rose, flowers from June

to August, and is 1 foot in height. The Himalayas are the hunting grounds for *Cyananthus lobatus*, azure-blue, flowering in July and August, and 3 inches in height. Its dainty blue colour is bearded with white. It must be kept well drained and moist. The popular name is also Cyananthus. The *Cyclamen* is the Sow Bread, and its species will thrive under the shadows of trees ; many of them flower from January to October, and are 3 inches in height. They should be in well-drained positions and prefer peat and leaf-mould. The colours of the flowers are white, rose, and crimson, and the foliage is sometimes marbled. *Cypripedium acaule* is the Lady's Slipper, rose-purple in colour, flowering during June and July and 1 foot in height. These are hardy orchids, and are really beautiful bulbous flowers, and thrive well where good drainage is afforded in shady moist positions. Amongst the species that can be grown on rockwork are the following, besides the one mentioned : *C. arietinum*, green and rose-coloured blossoms appearing in May and June, 6 inches; *C. calceolus*, yellow, May to July, 1 foot; *C. candidum*, brown and white, May and June, 9 inches; *C. macranthum*, purple, May to July, 6 inches; *C. parviflorum*, yellow, June and July, 1½ feet; *C. pubescens*, with yellow flowers also appearing from May to July, 1 foot; and *C. spectabile*, rose and white, appearing in blossom from June to August, and 1 foot in height.

Daphne blagayana—the Garland flower—is white in colour, flowers from March to May and is 6 inches in height. It is fragrant and as it blossoms so early in the year is a very desirable inhabitant of the garden rockery. Others, differing in colour and not exceeding a foot in height, are *D. cneorum*, rose-coloured, and *D. rupestris*, pink. They require partial shade and go on flowering from April until August. *Delphinium brunonianum*—the Larkspur—blue in colour and 1 foot in height, and *D. zalil* are recommended on account of their small size. The last-named has yellow flowers, blooms during June and July, and is 6 inches only in height, the flowering time of *D. brunonianum* being July and August. They are hardy and herbaceous plants. *Dianthus alpinus* — the Pink — has red blossom appearing in June and July, and is 6 inches in height. The genus may be described as consisting of sun-loving plants suitable for crevices in rocks or old walls, or for growing in pockets of the rockery. The colours, flowering times, and sizes of others of this most interesting family are: *D. cæsius* (commonly called the Cheddar pink) blossom pink, flowering time June and July, height, 3 inches; *D. deltoides*, red, June to September, 3 inches; *D. fischerii*, red, May to July, 3 inches; *D. Knappi*, yellow, August and September, 3 inches; and *D. tymphrastus*, crimson, June to August, 6 inches. A variety of *D. deltoides*, sub-named *albus*, is white, flowers from June to September, and is 3 inches in height.

Draba azoides—Whitlow grass—produces pretty evergreen tufts of leaves, has yellow flowers, blooms in April and May, is 3 inches high and well suited for the garden rockery.

A white-blossomed kind, flowering at the same time, is *D. maweana*, also 3 inches high; whilst *D. johannis* is also white, the same height, and begins flowering in March, going on to May.

Dryas drummondii — commonly called Dryas—produces yellow blossoms appearing in July and August, and is 3 inches high; whilst *D. octopetala* is white, flowers at the same time, is the same height and produces sheets of evergreen foliage. The last-named is called the "Mountain Avens." A rarer species, also white, blossoming in July and August, and 3 inches high, is *D. tenella*, which comes from Labrador. *Edrainthus* is a genus whose popular and botanical names are spelt the same way. It produces tufts of evergreen foliage, dense in habit, and bell-shaped blossoms. The following species make charming little rockery plants: *E. caricinus*, blue, June and July, 3 inches; *E. dalmaticus*, purple, June and July, 3 inches; *E. pumiliorum*, blue, May and June, 3 inches; *E. serpyllifoleus*, violet-purple, July and August,

2 inches in height. The leaves are thin, wiry, glaucous (sea-green or bluish tint) and the little plants thrive well in rocky crevices in sunny positions, but require plenty of moisture—the soil being gritty, stony, and the stones preferably limestone, quite easy to obtain. *Eomecon chionantha* has snow-white flowers, with yellow stamens, flowers from April to July, and is from 1 foot to 15 inches high. *Epilobium* is the generic name of the Willow Herb, most specimens of which are perhaps too large for the ordinary rockery; but the two following species are much smaller: *E. fleischerii*, rose colour, blossoming from June to August, 6 inches high; and *E. obcordatum* (loving a sunny position), pink in colour and 9 inches high. *Epimedium niveum*—Barrenwort—is white, and 1 foot high. *E. versicolor* is white and lilac, flowers from March to May, and is 9 inches in height. Their foliage is ornamental and they like a shady position. *Erinus*—popularly so called also—is a genus of pretty little rockery plants, which flower abundantly. *E. alpinus* is pur-

ple, and flowers from February to May; *E. alpinus-albus* is white, flowering from April to June; and *E. hispanicus* is pink, and flowers during April and May. All the three just named are 3 inches in height. *Gaultheria procumbens*—Partridge Berry—is an evergreen shrub. It has prostrate stems, bears white flowers, has scarlet berries in the autumn, and is suited either for growing under trees or in exposed positions on the rockery. Another species is *G. shallon,* which grows from 1 to 3 feet in height, and bears a pink flower. It flowers from June to September, and is desirable for planting in large compartments of big rockeries. *Gentiana acaulis*—commonly called the Gentian—is rich blue in colour, flowers from April to July, and is 3 inches high. It is very easily grown in strong loamy soil, "flavoured," so to speak, with limestone. The best position for it is where it can get morning sun. The following are desirable species: *G. acaulis alba,* white flowers, appearing in August and September, is 1 foot in height; *G. bavarica,* flowers blue, with small tufts of deep green leaves. It blossoms during April and May, and is only 3 inches high; *G. cruciata* has blue flowers, blossoming during June and July; and *G. verna*, also having tufts of deep green leaves, has bright blue flowers that appear in May and June, and it grows to a height of 2 inches. *Geranium* is the generic name of the Cranes Bill, and the following are very desirable species for garden rockery, namely: *G. argenteum*, so named because of its silvery foliage; its flowers are pink, it blossoms during June and July, and the plant is 1 foot high. *G. cinereum*, pink, flowering June and July, 6 inches; *G. lancastriense*, pink, flowering July and August, 3 inches; *G. macrorhizum*, purple, flowering same time, 1 foot, and *G. wallichianum*, red, July and August, 1 foot. *Gnaphalium leontopodium*—Cudweed—is better known as the "Edelweiss," an Alpine flower which is as easy to cultivate as it is beautiful, with its silky foliage and white, everlasting flowers. It likes a sunny position, flowers from July to

September, and is only 3 inches high. A good way to plant is by inserting the seeds in earthy crevices of the rockery, taking care to keep them moist during germination. Another species of the genus is *G. himalayanum*, which is even hardier than *G. leontopodium*. It flowers from June to July, and grows to a height of from 6 to 12 inches. *Haberlea* has no other common name than this, its botanical generic one, and *H. rhodopensis* has purple, bluish lilac, or mauve-purple blossoms, which appear during July and August, and makes a growth of from 3 to 6 inches. It likes a northern position that slopes on the rockery, that is, a position facing to the north. *Helianthemum pilosell-oides*—Sun Rose—is suitable for the drier and more open and exposed part of a rockery. The blossom is yellow, it appears during June and July, and is 6 inches high. *H. roseum* is rose-coloured in bloom, appears from June to August and is the same height. The following three are 9 inches high, flower from June to August, and their flowers are coloured as follows: *H. tuberaria*, yellow; *H. umbellatum*, white, producing dwarf masses of foliage, and *H. venustum*, scarlet. *Hepatica angulosa*—Liverwort—from its smallness, 9 inches high, is suitable for certain compartments of the garden rockery; its flowers are pale blue and appear in March and April. *H. triloba alba* has a white flower; *H. triloba cerulea* a blue one, and *H. triloba rubra* a red one. Each of the last three is 6 inches high—the two first-named of them flowering during March and April, and the last-named from February to April. *Hieraceum* is the generic name of the Hawkweed, and *H. villosum* bears yellow flowers in July and August, and is 1 foot high. *Hippocrepis comosa*—Horse-shoe Vetch—is a pretty trailing plant, with yellow flowers, produced from May to July, and is 3 inches high. *Hypericum coris*—St. John's Wort—has evergreen tufted foliage, yellow blossom coming out in August and September, and is 3 inches high. *H. nummularium* is yellow-blossomed, also flowers in June and July, and is the same height; whilst a particularly pretty species, *H. reptans*, with the same-coloured blossom appearing in July and August, 6 inches high, has bright green foliage. Not many lovers of gardens are there that do not know the pretty little Candytuft, but a smaller number are aware that the botanical generic name of the little plant is *Iberis*, and the following species are of the colours, times of flowering, and heights enumerated below: *I. corifolia*, white, April to July, 9 inches; *I. gibraltarica*, lilac, April to July, 9 inches; *I. jacunda*, pink, May to July, 6 inches; *I. petræa*, white, May to July, 3 inches; *I. sempervirens*, white, April and May, 3 inches. The recommendation of bright evergreen foliage is an addition to the qualification of the prettily-named Candytuft for the garden rockery. *Lavandula* is the generic name of the beautifully scented and familiar Lavender, and *L. compacta* is a small species, lavender in colour, flowering in July and August, and 18 inches in height. It would be a pretty and fragrant addition to rockery.

From garden rockery it is, perhaps, a " far

cry " to the Rocky Mountains, but the charm of garden culture of anything lies in its reminiscent suggestiveness of wild country. *Lewisia* is both the generic and the popular designation of a charming little plant that comes to us from the Rocky Mountains. It produces—that is to say the species *L. rediviva*—pretty little tufts of foliage from its tapering, long and " fleshy " roots, flowers during April and May, rich rose-coloured and pretty, crowning a plant 3 inches high; whilst another species, *L. tweedii*, is a North American congener, more rare, but equally interesting, whose flowers are pink—a rosy pink—blooming sometimes from June to August, and growing from 3 to 6 inches high. The first-named of these two species likes a sunny and warm position, but *L. tweedii* loves a somewhat shadier nook in the garden rockery. *Linaria alpina*—the Toad Flax—is another pretty rock plant, known as the Alpine Snapdragon. Its blossom is both blue and purple, appearing from June to August, and the plant is 6 inches high. The following are other species of this interesting genus: *L. cymbalaria*, has lilac flowers, and the plant is 3 inches high; *L. cymbalaria alba*, white ones; and *L. hepaticæfolia*, purple flowers—all three appearing from June to August, and each plant having a growth of 3 inches. *L. organifolia* is blue-flowered, blossoms from May to September, and is a foot high. *L. pallida* is purple in bloom, flowering also from May to September, and it is 3 inches high. *L. pilosa*, with purple flowers smaller than those of *L. pallida*, appears from June to September, and is 3 inches high; and *L. repens*—popularly called "Snowflake"—white, flowering at the same times; whilst *L. vulgaris peloria* has yellow flowers from July to September, and is 18 inches high.

Linnea borealis—Twin flower—botanically named, it is believed, after the great botanist Linnæus—because it was understood to be a favourite plant of his—has pretty trailing, evergreen leaves, and sweet-scented pink flowers, blooming from June to August, and is 3 inches high. It loves a cool and sandy peat soil, and hence a shady position. *Linum* is the generic name of the Flax, and *L. alpinum* bears blue flowers that appear during July and August and it is 6 inches high ; whilst *L. arboreum* has yellow flowers that appear during the same months and has a height of 1 foot. A very pretty species also is *L. flavum*, yellow-blossomed, flowering from May to September and 1 foot high.

The cry is " still they come " ; and from " all parts," crowding for admission to English garden rockeries ; and here are some fresh ones, which for brevity shall have their names, flowering time, and height, set out in consecutive order. *Lithospermum angustifolium*—Gromwell—yellow, June and July, 6 inches ; *L. canescens* (from America), yellow, June to August, 6 inches (a rather shady position suits it) ; *L. gastonii*, deep blue, June to August, 6 inches ; *L. graminifolium*, very beautiful, with grass-green, grass-like foliage (from northern Italy), deep blue, June to August, 1 foot, splendidly " shrubby," naturally growing on limestone rocks and hence preferring limestone soil or mortar refuse mixed with limestone soil, and a sunny, well-drained position ; *L. intermedium*, blue, June and July, 1 foot ; *L. petræum*, azure-blue, May to August (from Dalmatia), a foot and three quarters, liking a sunny aspect, well drained in deep, sandy soil ; *L. prostratum*, deep blue, preferring a northerly or north-westerly sheltered position, of spreading habit and requiring room for its pretty foliage and flowers to hang pendent over rockery stones, or it could be planted in crevices of the rockery stones in a mixture of loam and peat ; and finally there is *L. purpureo-cærulea*, with purple and blue flowers appearing from May to July and growing to a height of 6 inches. We must not forget *Lotus corniculatus*—the well-known and prettily named Bird's-foot trefoil, freely flowering, trailing, with yellow blossoms appearing from June to August, and 3 inches in height. Nor must we forget the pretty Campion—of which the following species are suitable for rockery compartments or pockets on account of their size being less than some of the species: *Lychnis alpina*, pink blossom, April to June, 6 inches; *L. alpina-alba*, white, April to June, 6 inches; *L. flos-cuculi-alba*, white, June to August, 1 foot; *L. flos-cuculi rosea*, rosy pink, June to August, 1 foot; *L. fulgens*, scarlet, June to August, 1 foot; *L. haageana hybrida*, pink, scarlet, and other colours, June to August, 1 foot; *L. lagascæ*, rose, June to August, 3 inches; *L. viscaria*, rose-red, June to August, 9 inches. The following two species: *L. viscaria-alba*, white, and *L. viscaria splendens*, rose, also appear from June to August, and are 9 inches high. *Lysimachia capitata*—the Loose-strife—has yellow flowers appearing during June and July, and is 1 foot high. *L. nummularia* is yellow-blossomed, flowers June to August, and is 6 inches high; whilst *L. nummularia aurea* is the Moneywort, flowers from June to August, and is also 6 inches high. And now we come to our well-known friend the Poppy-resembling *Meconopsis*, and must mention two of the smaller kinds as specially suitable for rockery. These are *M. cambrica*, yellow, June to August, 1 foot, and *M. cambrica flora plena*, yellow, June to August, and 1 foot, whilst one 2-feet specimen, flowering the same times, is *M. wallichii.*

Mesembryanthemum unciniatum is as curious as is the length of its generic botanical name, which, however, appears to be its only popular one. It is a hardy, what is called "succulent" plant, having thick, fleshy, curiously jointed stems. It thrives in a sheltered sunny position on the rockery, but must not be too damp, and sandy loam with small broken pieces of stone is a suitable soil for it. Its flowers are pink. *Mitchella repens*, which is popularly called Mitchella, is an evergreen, creeping little plant, that comes from North America; it has white flowers, produced from May to July, succeeded by scarlet berries, and its height is 3 inches. A boggy position is best for it, made up in the shade with soil of sandy leaf-mould. *Morisia hypogæa*, popularly called Morisia, has yellow blossoms; it flowers during May and June, possesses rosettes of foliage, which is evergreen, is 3 inches in height, and is of easy culture if given a south aspect and planted in deep, well-drained, sandy loam, mixed with fragments of stony grit. The common name suggests that we should not overlook the pretty and well-known Forget-me-not, which is generically *Myosotis*, and the following species are well suited to the garden rockery: *M. alpestris*, bright blue, flowering in April and May, 3 inches high; *M. azorica*, dark blue, May to August, 6 inches; *M. dissitiflora*, blue, April to June, 3 inches; *M. palustris*, blue, May to August, 6 inches; *M. rehsteineri*, blue, April to June, 4 inches; *M. rupicola*, blue, April and May, 3 inches; *M. sylvatica*, blue, April and May, 1 foot; and *M. sylvatica alba*, white, April and May, 1 foot. A most curious and interesting plant is the Evening Primrose, generically called *Œnothera*, whose smaller species are well adapted for the rockery. *Œ. eximea* has white flowers, produced from June to September, and is 6 inches high. *Œ. macrocarpa*, yellow,

June to August, 6 inches. *Œ. riparia*, yellow, June to September, 1 foot. *Œ. speciosa*, white, May to August, 1 foot. *Œ. speciosa-rosea*, rose-coloured, June to August, 1 foot. *Œ. taraxacifolia*, white, June to August, 6 inches. *Omphalodes luciliæ* is the creeping Forget-me-not, and comes from Asia Minor. At first the flowers are pink, and then change to blue. It blossoms from April to August, and is a charming little plant 3 inches in height. It loves a sunny position on the rockery in sandy loam and peat, with fragments of broken stone or grit. Shade is also desirable, and a certain protection from cutting wind. Other species of this genus are *O. nitida*, blue-flowered, from June to August, 6 inches high; *O. verna*, free-growing and trailing, flowers blue, height 6 inches; and *O. verna-alba*, white, flowers trailing, March to May, 6 inches high. *Ononis rotundifolia* is the Rest Harrow, has pink blossoms, appearing from June to August, and is 1 foot high. It is easily grown, and will thrive on the drier and rougher parts of the rockery.

Onosma alba-rosea is white and pink, blossoms from May to September, and is 6 inches high. It likes a cool and moist position. *O. taurica* has yellow flowers, is suited for a dry and sunny position, free from too much moisture. The blossoms are produced in clusters from May to September, are almond-scented, and the plant (which comes to us from Greece) grows from 6 inches to a foot high. *O. thompsonii* is carmine in colour when in bloom, flowers from May to September, the plant being 1 foot high. *Opuntia arborescens* is the Indian Fig, a hardy succulent plant with purple flowers arriving during June and July, and it is 3 feet high; but *O. rafinesquiana* and *O. camanchia* both have yellow flowers from June to July, and each is 1 foot high. They require a well-drained position. Of the *Orchis* genus there are three suitable for boggy positions. The handsome green foliage is purple-spotted. *O. foliosa* has purple flowers, is in bloom during June and July, and is 18 inches high. *O. maculata* has lilac and purple flowers in June and July, and is 1 foot in height; whilst *O. maculata superba* shows its purple blossoms during the same period and grows to a height of 18 inches. *Orobus* is the Bitter Vetch, and the following are respectively the colours, times of flowering, and heights of the several species: *O. alpestre*, pink, April and May, 1 foot; *O. aurantius*, orange, April to June, 1 foot; *O. canescens*, blue, June and July, 1 foot; *O. cyanus*, blue, June and July, 1 foot; *O. lathyroides*, purple-blue, June and July, 18 inches; *O. niger*, purple, June and July, 2 feet; *O. varius*, red, June and July, 1 foot; *O. vernus*, red, April and May, 1 foot; *O. vernus albus*, white, April and May, 1 foot; and *O. vernus plenus*, white, June and July, 1 foot. *Oxalis* is the pretty and well-known Wood Sorrel, and *O. enneaphylla* has white blossoms, flowers from June to August, and is 6 inches high. Its foliage is silvery and glaucous, and a warm position with sandy loam soil is what it delights in. And now for a brief reference to the handsome and interesting Poppy—*Papaver* genus—and mention of some various-coloured species that will be an ornament to garden rockery. They rejoice in a sunny position, with small stones mixed in the soil. These are *P. alpinum*, yellow, June to August, 6 inches; *P. alpinum-album*, white, June to August, 6 inches; *P. alpinum-miniatum*, orange, June to August, 3 inches; *P. alpinum-roseum*, rose, June to August, 3 inches; and the following, though larger, are very handsome adjuncts to the rockery: *P. bracteatum*, scarlet, June to August, 3 feet high; *P. nudicaule*, yellow, May to August, 1 foot; *P. nudicaule album*, white, May to August, 1 foot; and *P. nudicaule miniatum*, orange, May to August, 1 foot. The grass of Parnassus is represented by three species which are very striking, especially the third mentioned, *Parnassia asarifolia*, white, June and July, 6 inches; *P. nubicola*, white, June and July, 1 foot; *P. palustris*, white, June and July, 6 inches. *Petrocallis pyrenaica* is commonly called by its generic name, has sweet-scented, pale lilac-coloured flowers, produced during May and June, and is 3 inches high. Canary grass,

Phalaris arundinacea, is handsome and variegated, and though 4 feet high, would be suitable for a big "compartment" of a large rockery. Mention must not be overlooked of the genus *Phlox*, whose common name is the same as the generic one. They are dwarf creeping plants, which will quickly cover the compartment of rockery in which they are placed. Well-drained common soil and a sunny position suit them, and these are some of the numerous species: *P. amœna*, pink, April to June, 6 inches; *P. canadensis*, lilac, April and May, 9 inches; *P. canadensis alba*, white, April and May, 1 foot; *P. nivalis*, white, April to June, 3 inches; *P. pilosa*, pink, May and June, 9 inches; *P. procumbens*, pale purple, May and June, 6 inches; and there is a considerable list of sub-species under *P. setacea*, with a varied display of colours. A well-drained and sunny position will suit these handsome plants.

Phyteuma charmelii—the Rampion—has blue flowers, June and July, 6 inches; and *P. comosum* has also blue flowers; they appear in June. It is 6 inches in height. *Potentilla alba*—Cinquefoil—has white flowers, which appear in May and June, and the plant is 6 inches high. *P. ambigua* has yellow flowers appearing in July and August, and the plant is 6 inches high, whilst *P. argentea* has very beautiful silvery foliage and yellow flowers, produced also in July and August.

And now we come to the Primrose. Who can want anything better than this beautiful flower as a wilding? What can be more delightful and sweetly reminiscent than this charming plant as we see it in our English woods and lanes? But there are no doubt many people who admire it dyed with garden colours produced by domestication, so to speak; and for these, therefore, we will give a list of some, and they will come under the generic expression of *Primula*, and the specific designations which more or less denote their variations or departures from the normal form and colour of the wild plant *Primula vulgaris*. They are mostly small, ranging from 3 inches to a foot, although height has not much application to a plant whose leaves spread and lap. As the flowering time is pretty much the same, extending from March to July, we will just name the species and the colours of varieties that the cultivator may like to put on his garden rockery. Here then is the list : *P. admontensis*, purple ; *P. allionii*, rose-purple ; *P. auricula*, yellow ; *P. capitata*, deep blue ; *P. cashmiriana*, light purple ; *P. cashmiriana alba*, white ; *P. clusiana*, crimson ; *P. denticulata*, lilac ; *P. farinosa*, rose ; *P. floribunda*, clear yellow ; *P. floribunda isabellina*, sulphur ; *P. glutinosa*, blue-purple; *P. integrifolia*, pale rose; *P. intermedia*, violet ; *P. kitaibeliana*, rosy lilac ; *P. parryi*, purple-crimson ; *P. poissonii*, rosy mauve ; *P. rosea-grandiflora*, carmine-crimson ; and *P. scotica*, red. Damp, loamy soil will suit all the primulas. Note how and where the common primrose thrives best, and copy these conditions, and success will not be far off. *Pulmonaria* is the Lungwort. *P. angustifolia*, has blue flowers that appear during April and May, and is 1 foot high. *P. arvensis alba*, a white flower, April to June, 6 inches high. *P. azurea*, blue, March and April, 6 inches; and *P. saccharata* has prettily mottled pink flowers that come out in May and June, and it is 1 foot high. The well-known Feverfew, with golden foliage and white flowers, is *Pyrethrum*, and two of the species suitable for rockery are *P. parthenium* and *P. uliginosum*, flowering from July to October. Easily cultivated rock plants are the Ramondias, four of which, all flowering from June to August, are of the colours and heights now mentioned: *Ramondia nataliæ*, purple, 4 inches; *R. pyrenaica*, purple, 4 inches; *R. pyrenaica alba*, white, 4 inches; and *R. serbica*, lilac-blue colour, and four inches in height. We must not omit our Buttercups, generally called *Ranunculus*. The common Buttercups of our fields, one of the most abundant of which is *R. repens*, beautiful as they are when revelling in the wealth of their golden glory, are marvellously "energetic," so to speak, and rapidly cover spaces of ground and crowd out more delicate and less "progressive" plants; but we should, nevertheless, like to see large compartments of our own rockeries filled by various species of this delightful genus. For those, however, whose rockery space may be limited, there are smaller kinds than most of our native ones, and these we will briefly mention, premising that although infinite trouble may be taken to provide varying soils in different rockery compartments to suit what may be called the idiosyncrasies of different species, a great deal of success in cultivation may be obtained by just observing the " likings " of the common Buttercup and giving a moist, well-drained position in good sandy loam, mixed with that essential vegetable soil called leaf-mould. *R. alpestris* has white blossoms that come from May to July, and it is only 3 inches high. It is—as its specific name indicates—an Alpine plant. Its tufts of dark green foliage are very pretty. *R. anemonoides* is also white-blossomed, in flower during May and June, and 6 inches high; and the following are the colours, flowering time, and height of others of moderate size: *R. bullatus*, yellow, 9 inches; *R. glacialus*, pale pink, June and July, 6 inches; *R. graminifolius*, yellow, April and May, 9 inches; *R. montanus*, yellow, June and July, 6 inches; *R. parnassifolius*, white (from the Alps and Pyrenees), June and July, 6 inches; *R. rutæfolius*, yellow, April and May, 9 inches; and finally *R. seguieri*, white, May and June, 6 inches high.

Amongst what are called "old-fashioned flowers"—and personally let us say that, in horticulture, we greatly prefer the old-fashioned to the new-fashioned growths—is the sweet-scented Rosemary—*Rosmarius officinalis;* and although that delightful plant grows to a height of three feet, we would still find a place for it in a compartment of our rockery; but there is a smaller form, *R. officinalis prostrata*, 3 inches in height, to suit a smaller space. Both species have purple flowers, and both come into blossom during June and July. For a change from many other forms and hues of leafage, the Sage—*Salvia argentea*—with its silvery woolly leaves and yellow blossoms, should find a place in some convenient compartment. The name Soapwort—*Saponaria*—will come up amongst plants remembered in our mental category of wildings; and here are some small species deserving a place in garden rockery: *S. cæspitosa* has red blossoms and tufts of foliage; it flowers from June to August, and is 6 inches high. *S. lutea* is pale yellow, flowers from May to July, and is 3 inches high; *S. ocymoides* is pink, flowers in June and July, and is 9 inches high; *S. ocymoides-alba* has white blossoms, and *S. ocymoides splendidissima* rosy crimson ones; each of the two last-mentioned little plants, 3 inches high, is in blossom from May to August. *Sarracenia purpurea* is the American pitcher plant, and has curious leaves that are horn-like in appearance, rather broad in proportion to their height, which is from 6 to 12 inches. Another species of the same genus for growing on rockery is *S. psittacina*, which has yellowish blossoms, flowers at the same time, and is 6 inches high;

and yet another, 1 foot high, red blossom, flowering from May to July, is *S. variolaris;* whilst *S. rubra*, also red, is 18 inches high. The genus *Saxifraga*, whose species are commonly called Saxifrages, is a very large one, especially well suited, from the convenient smallness of their size, for growing on garden rockery. Most of them are easy to grow on almost any soil, but preferably on limestone soil; and it is important to plant them in crevices, out of which they can hang down in a slanting position, so that water may not rest on and rot the pretty foliage. Naturally they grow on limestone rocks, and hence the suggested soil. The mossy ones must not be placed in too sunny a position, as mossiness, as the least observant will have noticed, is generally found in at least partially shaded and moist positions. The general list is so long that we must select those differing in colour, and race through them. *S. affinis*, white (mossy), July to September, 3 inches; *S. aizoides*, yellow, July to September, 6 inches; *S. aizoon*, requiring a sunny position, white, June and July, 6 inches; *S. aizoon-compacta*, white-spotted, May to July, 3 inches; *S. altissima*, white, May to July, 6 inches (the leaves forming large rosettes); *S. aretioides*, yellow, June to August, 3 inches; *S. balkana*, pink, May and June, 6 inches; *S. blepharophylla*, rose, April to June, 3 inches; *S. burseriana*, white, and *S. boydii*, yellow, flowering during March and April, the first-named 6 inches and the second one 3 inches high, prefer a calcareous or chalky soil; *S. cotyledon*, white, June to August, 1 foot, likes a sunny position; *S. geum-crenata*, puce-coloured and spotted, 1 foot high; *S. griesbachi* (from Macedonia), purplish red, May and June, 3 inches; *S. longifolia*, has white blossoms in June and July, is 1 foot high, and likes a sunny position, whilst the following delight in shade: *S. oppositifolia*, rose, March and April, 2 inches or less; *S. o. alba*, white, and *S. o. major*, red, each flowering March and April, and 3 inches high; *S. o. pyrenaica*, rose, and *S. o. splendens*, rosy crimson, flower, the first May and June, the second March and April, and each is 3 inches high; *S. umbrosa* is bluish white, flowers from April to June, and is 1 foot high. *Schizocodon soldanelloides* is the Japanese Moonwort, has pink flowers, appearing from March to June, is 6 inches high, and is a delightful little plant, which loves a shady position.

And now comes the well-known Stonecrop, in its wild English form so delightfully spread upon many a rock and old wall. Its generic name is *Sedum,* and gardeners usually refer to the various species as "Sedums." Indispensable as they are for any rockery, our space will only admit of mention of a few having distinctive colours: *S. acre,* yellow, June and July, 3 inches; *S. album,* white, July to September, 3 inches; *S. anacampseros,* purple, July and August, 6 inches; *S. anglicum,* white and red, July and August, 6 inches; *S. kamtschaticum,* orange, June to August, 6 inches; *S. lydium* (having very bright green foliage), pink blossom, June and July, 3 inches; *S. sempervivoides,* red, June and

July, 6 inches (this one has little fleshy rosettes of leaves), and *S. sieboldii*, blush, June to August, 3 inches. Who has not admired the fleshy stability of the common Houseleek, which so often is found thriving and, so to speak, fattening on the rubbly, half-decayed tops of old walls, and revelling in the dank parts of half-rotten thatch where leaf-soil has accumulated? Here, then, let us introduce them, under their botanical generic name of *Sempervivum*, for "service," if we may so phrase it, on our garden rockery; and again, as the list is so long, we must restrict it by mentioning only those differing in colour. They are most interesting and quaint little plants, suitable for old walls—which are, of course, rockery—and dry banks. The striking general feature is the rosette form of the fleshy leaves. *S. arachnoideum*, purple, June and July, 6 inches; *S. globiferum*, yellow, June and July, 6 inches; *S. hirtum*, white, June and July, 6 inches; *S. laggerii*, cobwebby in appearance, red, May and June, 3 inches; *S. pittonii*, stone colour, July and

August, 6 inches; *S. powellii* (cobwebby), purple, June and July, 9 inches; *S. reginæ amaliæ*, purple, with bronze-coloured rosettes, margined thickly with hairs; and finally, *S. triste*, purple, and of a rich metallic colour; flowering in May and June, and 6 inches high. Don't let us forget our familiar friend the wild Groundsel, beloved of birds, and exhibiting, especially in all rich garden soil, the most marvellous vigour and having a most amazing tendency to spread everywhere. Its botanical name is *Senecio*, and the smallest of the species is *S. doronicum*, yellow-blossomed from June to August, 1 foot in height. A larger kind, with purple-crimson flowers on a plant 2 feet high, flowering in September and October, is *S. pulcher*. *Shortia galacifolia* has only the common name of *Shortia*. It is a beautiful little plant, 6 inches high, introduced from America, and has white flowers, produced in May and June, likes a damp, shady position on light loamy or peaty soil, and requires plenty of watering. Another species, with rose-coloured blossoms, coming into open flower from May to July, is *S. uniflora*, an importation from Japan. *Silene acaulis* is the Catchfly. It has small, moss-like, tufted, rose-coloured flowers, opening in June and July, and the plant is 2 inches or less in height. Other species are: *S. alpestris*, white, May to July, 9 inches; *S. maritima*, having prostrate tufts of glaucous foliage, and white flowers appearing during July and August: it is 3 inches high; *S. pennsylvanica*, red, June and July, 6 inches; *S. pumilio*, rose, June and July, 6 inches; *S. schafta*, rose-purple, April to June, 6 inches; and *S. virginica*, which is a native of North America, and very hardy, having crimson flowers appearing during June and July, and 18 inches high. A soil poor but gritty will suit them generally, but *S. pumilio* likes a better one, loamy, sandy, and peaty, as well as "gritty."

Soldanella alpina, popularly called Soldanella, is a pretty little plant, of Alpine origin, as its specific name suggests. It has shining foliage, produced in evergreen tufts, pendent purple flowers, opening in April and May, and is 3 inches high. *S. montana* is also purple-flowered, blossoms in April, and is 3 inches high. *S. pusilla*, purple-blue flowers, April and May, 2 inches, and *S. pyrolæfolia*, also purple-blue, flowering the same time, and 3 inches high. Crevices in the stones of the garden rockery will suit them, and ordinary soil with a mixture of sandy peat, and a cool and moist position well drained. Just a brief mention of one species of the Golden Rod—*Solidago virgaurea nana*—which from its size, 1 foot high, is available for the garden rockery. Its flowers are yellow and appear in September. Three species of the Meadow Rue—*Thalictrum*—may also, on account of their pretty fern-like foliage, be recommended for the adornment of a rockery. *T. adiantifolium* has white flowers, which appear during June and July; the plant is 9 inches high. *T. anemenoides* has also white blossom; this comes out in April and May, and is 6 inches high. *T. delavayi* has rose flowers in June and July, and is 18 inches high; and

T. minus is purple, flowers during June and July, and is 6 inches high. *Thymus azoricus* —Thyme—must not be forgotten. It has a purple flower, appearing from June to August, and is 6 inches high. Of this pretty genus suitable for a rockery and forming carpets of evergreen foliage, are the following: *T. citriodorus argenteus*, and *aureus*, lilac, both flowering June to August, and 6 inches high, and the under-named all flowering during June and July; *T. corsicus*, lilac, 2 inches; *T. lanuginosus* and *T. micans nanus*, both purple, 6 and 3 inches high respectively; *T. serpyllum*, rose-coloured, 6 inches; *T. serpyllum-album*, white, 6 inches; and *T. serpyllum coccineus*, crimson, 3 inches. The pretty little Foam flower—*Tiarella cordifolia* —with its erect, feathery plumes of white blossoms, is 6 inches high, and may also be introduced on garden rockery. And now come to be mentioned the wood lilies, which rejoice in moist, shady positions, and whose colours, times of flowering, and sizes are as follows: *Trillium cernuum*, white, May and June, 9 inches; *T. erectum*, dark purple, April and May, 9 inches; *T. erythrocarpum*, white and rose, May and June, 9 inches; *T. grandiflorum-roseum*, rose, May and June, 6 inches; *T. ovatum*, white, May and June, 6 inches; *T. sessile*, brown, April and May, 6 inches; *T. sessile-californicum*, creamy white, April and May, 6 inches; and *T. stylosum*, rose, May and June, 6 inches. A general recommendation of the pretty Speedwells—*Veronica*—for the rockery is the quickness with which they will trail upon or otherwise cover the compartments of rockery in which they are placed; and of these we will just mention and briefly describe the colours, flowering time, and heights of half a dozen species that will grow and thrive in almost any soil. These are V. *bidwelli*, white, July and August, 6 inches; *V. incana*, blue, July to September, 2 feet; *V. repens*, blue and white, June and July, 3 inches; *V. rupestris*, blue, June and July, 3 inches; *V. spicata*, blue, August and September, 1 foot; and *V. spicata-alba*, white, June and July, 1 foot; and finally in this chapter we must mention our dear little friend the Violet. It is not necessary to introduce to the rockery lover the beautiful native wildings *Viola canina*, *V. hirta*, *V. odorata*, *V. palustris*, or *V. tricolor*, respectively known as the dog, the hairy, the sweet, and the marsh Violets, and the Pansy, all of which should be welcome ; but merely to suggest the addition to them of the following : *V. pedata*, blue, flowering in May and June, 6 inches high, and *V. pedata-bicolor*, violet and blue, appearing also in May and June, and 3 inches high.

IX

HEDGE-BANKS AND OLD WALLS

IN many a garden, especially in the country, part of the boundary consists of a hedge or an old wall, and there are illimitable possibilities of turning these into dreams of beauty. If the cynic should say: "You profess to be a lover of Nature: why then do you not leave your hedge-bank or your old wall as you find it, a tangle of grass, ivy, nettles, brambles, and other rankly-luxuriant vegetation?"—our reply is that in this country the majority of the landscapes are not Nature purely and simply, beautiful as wild, unadulterated Nature always is, but Nature spoilt by man. The clearance of its primeval woods by its inhabitants for the building of towns and the establishment of farms has modified the country so much that all we can usually see is Nature struggling to regain possession of the fields and woods, and of the long mounds of earth thrown up by the agriculturist for divisional purposes and called "hedges." In most districts "the hedger and ditcher," with billhook and spade, periodically cuts back and disfigures the free wild growths which unfettered Nature would make in the course of one short year.

We remember, however, reading some years ago a description of an unlet, neglected farm, whose fields were a blaze of colour and beauty. In the whole of England there is perhaps only one forest—the New Forest, in Hampshire—"new" no longer—in parts of which the landscapes are indescribably lovely; where at certain seasons the glades and dells over wide areas are golden with gorse and purple with blossoming heather, and the copses are dyed with the blue of the wild hyacinth and resplendent with a carpet of flowering primroses, whilst the glades are covered with inimitable grace by the presence of waving bracken; and it is quite permissible, so long as Nature is not outraged by our processes, to gather around us, in our little microcosms of it, just those features that strike our fancy. We can remove dead leaves from spots where they are piled at the annual " fall," and fill the spaces at once with living forms of beauty—thus merely anticipating Nature's slower methods.

To make our meaning quite clear we will illustrate in the following pages what we propose. Our engraving No. 23 (page 137) is from a photograph of a bit of wild hedge-side, showing the graceful form of the Soft prickly Shield fern growing out from a tangle of ivy and other crowded greenery. The dead fronds of the previous year hang down below it. In time these would rot and form leaf-mould, and the more vigorous of the plants forming the green mass of the bank would stifle those underneath, and the latter, in time, would become vegetable earth and enrich the soil of the hedge ; but the cultivator could at once remove the superfluous vegetation, leaving the fern where it is, and fill up all the slanting space with other wild plants he may like—that is to say, plants that he finds growing elsewhere upon similar soil in similar positions. En-

23. A bit of wild hedge-side, showing Soft Prickly Shield Fern (page 136).

graving No. 24 (page 139) gives another little wild hedge-bank picture, showing another view of a Soft prickly Shield fern standing out from a background of ivy and dead sprays of grass. These could be removed, and some of the ivy, in places where the latter was too crowded, and showed a tendency to choke other and smaller growths that it might be desired to encourage by more space, more air, and more sunshine; and room could also be found for the introduction of other small wildings suited to the more shady or more sunny positions.

A further illustration is furnished by engraving No. 25 (page 139). The prominent figure in this little picture is again the very beautiful *Polystichum angulare*, that, having had more opportunity for spreading itself, is seen to occupy nearly all the space. Here also is a dense "tangle" of living and dead things—grass, underneath, and tendrils, some green and others decayed, of bramble. Some of the fern fronds have got blown "awry" by the wind, and may be found broken or

24. Another view of hedge-side and Soft Prickly Shield Fern
(page 138).

25. Yet another bit of hedge-side and Soft Prickly Shield Fern
(page 138).

otherwise damaged. These and the dead things, and a good bit of the living tangle, could be removed; and there would thus be found room for a clump or two of primroses, and one or two small hartstongue ferns, which love to grow and are often found growing mixed with the charming Shield ferns.

Another "patch" of hedge-bank, photographed exactly as it was found, is shown by engraving No. 26 (page 141). This represents a pretty tangle of Common *Polypody, Polypodium vulgare*, Black maidenhair Spleenwort, *Asplenium adiantum-nigrum*, and ivy; and it will be seen that these three are practically occupying nearly all the space, and are so naturally and charmingly mingled as to require no alteration, unless it be to remove some of the dead "sprays" of other things shown at the bottom of the picture, or to assist Nature by removing a dead ivy leaf or a dead fern frond; and to remove a leaf or frond where, in places, one shows a disposition to too vigorously overgrow its companion.

26. A pretty tangle of Ferns (page 140).

27. Hedge-bank, with Common Polypody (page 142).

The beautifully evergreen Common *Polypody* occupies, it will be seen, a prominent share in the patch of hedge-bank pictured in engraving No. 27 (page 141). Thrusting out its pendent fronds—to catch the incidence of sunlight—it provides a delightful foil to the mossy shadow of the bank behind. At the right-hand top side of the picture a leaf or two of holly will be seen—the dark-eyed beauty that lends so much evergreen loveliness to English hedge-banks. There is not much that could be done to fill up this picture except, perhaps, to insert in the mossy background at spots that would be reached by sunshine some time during the day, a patch or two of pennywort, to add, by its brightness, to the refreshing verdancy of the mossy bank.

Yet another aspect, in engraving No. 28 (page 143) of the Common Polypody, at a spot where it is struggling chiefly with ivy—and successfully—for the mastery. All that the cultivator could do here is to look carefully and lovingly over the spot, and removing a dead leaf here and a dead spray there—helping Nature in fact in its never-ending effort to promote the "survival of the fittest." The most energetic and obtrusive of all hedge-side shrubs is the prickly and energetic

28. Another peep of hedge-bank showing Common Polypody (page 142).

bramble. Its well-meant efforts must sometimes be modified, and, in any case, it is always a relief to the vegetable inhabitants of the hedge to remove the numerous dead sprays of bramble. These get sometimes almost inextricably entwined amongst the living growths; and, in removing them, care must be taken to prevent the thorns, still active and aggressive, although on dead and brittle branches, from tearing the delicate fern fronds, mangling the sweet primrose leaves, or beheading a speedwell or herb robert.

And now the beautiful Hartstongue—*Scolopendrium vulgare*—comes in for a share of notice in engraving No. 29 (page 145). It, too, is asserting its prominent evergreen loveliness by standing out prominently from a background of ivy and a more or less tangled mass, including dead sprays and tiny bits, of Common Polypody. Here the tender hand of the Nature-lover could remove a few of the less interesting growths that go to make up the tangle and supply their places by suitable substitutes.

Once more the Hartstongue comes to the front—in engraving No. 30 (page 145), by quite a blaze, so to speak, of delightful verdancy. The omnipresent ivy is still to be

29. Hartstongue in hedge-bank (page 144).

30. Another peep of hedge-bank and Hartstongue (page 144).

seen nestling at the back, but there are little spots covered by the tangle where desirable clearance could be made and some favourites of the cultivator introduced. Friendly help can also be given to the principal inhabitant

31. Male Fern standing out from a tangle of ivy (page 147).

—which otherwise should not be interfered with—by the removal of broken, insect-eaten, decayed or otherwise redundant parts—to the relief of the hartstongue itself.

Although one of the commonest and most

widely distributed of our native ferns, the Common Buckler fern, or as it is also called, because of its robust, virile appearance, the "Male fern," is a striking and graceful adornment to many a hedge-side and embankment. Engraving No. 31 (page 146) shows it, standing out boldly from a tangle, chiefly of ivy. If possessing such a hedge as a boundary to his garden, and there is plenty of other space, the cultivator might be disposed to think that the picture, as it is, is pretty enough. If he desires more variety and more colour as a contrast to the varying shades of green provided by the fern and the ivy, he can remove some of the latter ; but to deprive the former of any of its fronds would disturb the "balance" of its symmetry.

In the next engraving, No. 32 (page 148), the Male fern is again presented, and is again the crowning feature of the "bit" of ivied hedge-bank which it graces. One amongst scores of possible variations from the simple beauty of this little picture might be made by a flanking of primroses, violets, and that sweet early buttercup, the Lesser Celandine that

> Comes before the Swallow dares,
> To touch the winds of March with beauty.

32. Male Fern gracefully displaying itself in a hedge (page 147).

And curiously enough, after writing the preceding lines, including our illustrative suggestion, we refer to dear old Wordsworth, and find what we had read before, but for the moment had forgotten—that he associates these very three wild flowers in the lines :—

> Long as there's a sun that sets
> Primroses will have their glory;
> Long as there are violets,
> They will have a place in story.

And then he continues :—

> There's a flower that shall be mine,
> 'Tis the little Celandine.

The next illustration is not of an old wall, but of quite a new one, or one comparatively new, near the top of which is a crevice, accidentally left and damp. A pretty little Hartstongue has established itself—engraving No. 33 (page 150). It was, to the best of our recollection, either a limestone or hard red sandstone wall, by a roadside in Devon, that we saw this bonny-looking and courageous fern, and it was adding so much beauty to the otherwise naked barrenness of the wall that we were tempted to photograph it, and give it such modest immortality as this

33. A pretty little Hartstongue has established itself on a new wall (page 149).

volume may afford. We passed the same wall only a few days before writing this chapter and found that some selfish and ruthless tourist had removed it. He, or she, was doubtless quite bereft of any poetic

34. Some venturesome little plants have established themselves in this bit of stone-bank (page 152).

sentiment, and we are therefore glad that we have preserved the portrait of the little plant.

And now for one or two little pictures of bits of hedge mended by stone. Engraving No. 34 (page 151) shows the tangle of greenery, chiefly grass, above and below the stonework. The hedge-maker has, of course, had no thought of planting anything in the stony crevices, nor has the idea of doing so occurred to his employer—the farmer. Nevertheless, some venturesome little plants—we forget what they were—have established themselves, through the agency of their seed, in the earthy interstices. Here, then, is a field for the garden owner and rockery lover who may find his property, newly acquired, furnished with such a wall, to remove the grass above and below the stonework, and utilise that and the stony crevices for growing some suitable plants selected from the long list in the preceding chapter, and thus adding great beauty to this little site.

Here is another piece of mended hedge—engraving No. 35 (page 153)—adjoining a gate photographed just as we found it. Being new work, no growths have been insinuated into the crevices; and the rest of the bank shown consists of grass and other rank growths; but here again the possibilities of

35. The possibilities for ornamenting this bit of new stonework will be obvious (page 152).

ornamentation will be obvious. The garden lover who chanced to buy or rent any place so bounded might easily turn the utilitarian wires into a trellis of wires, and by preparing and planting the hedge-top with climbing plants might turn the uninteresting adjunct into a garden of delight.

36. Bank, stonework, and fence capable of obvious transformation.

Again, engraving No. 36 (above) represents another haphazard bit of fence. The immediate foreground is simply a sloping grass bank leading up to the stonework. How delightful to transplant there any bank-loving wild flowers, or alpine or other flowers

37. A bit of old wall inviting improvement (page 157).

on the slope, using the almost exhaustive list in the preceding chapter to select from ! The commonplace wooden fence could be masked by trailing, flowering plants, or by tendrils of ivy ; and roots of anything suitable pressed into the stony crevices ; and thus three different "sets" of effects could be produced on bank, stonework, and fence.

Engraving No. 37 (page 155) represents a bit of older wall, in the crevices of which moss is growing and some other tiny growths, whilst the upper part of the wall is mantled with ivy. As an example for "followers," a bold dandelion has fixed itself in the centre of the wall, and was in full blossom when we photographed it, although it is necessarily rather inconspicuous in the print. Here again is a basis for ornamentation ; and, if nothing better for masking such a wall is available, sprays of ivy could be planted at the foot of it and trained upon it, or seeds of rock-loving plants requiring little soil could be mixed with soft pieces of loam and pressed into the crevices.

Along the top of the wall, pictured by engraving No. 38 (page 157), a lot of earth had been banked up, out of which hawthorn and ivy had grown. The stony crevices were filled with moss, and in the centre, crowning the wall, a little patch of pennywort, which can be easily seen by a magnifying glass, had established itself as a sort of suggestion of what might be added to redeem the otherwise bald appearance of the wall.

38. Hedge and old wall inviting the rockery lover to improve it (page 156).

Here, finally, for the purposes of this chapter, is a little perspective of stone steps, No. 39 (below); this, one may not unfrequently

39. The wild tangle flanking the steps awaits adornment.

find leading up from one terrace to another of a garden. The bank on either side of the steps is simply a tangle, chiefly of grass; but how delightful to plant rock flowers on the banks and in the angles of the steps. The picture really represents the access from a water lane to a private meadow, and the stile at the top is there to prevent cattle straying from the meadow; but the reader needs only to omit the stile to give the position its full amount of suggestiveness.

X

THE BIG AND THE SMALL ROCKERY

THE size of a garden rockery will, of course, entirely depend upon the space at the disposal of the cultivator, and upon his means. The method of building will be the same. It is all a question of proportion.

Our illustrations in this chapter will be of big rockeries, and we are indebted to the courtesy of Mr. Peter Veitch, J.P., head of the well-known firm of Robert Veitch & Co., of the Royal Nurseries, Exeter, whence originated the business which has made the name of Veitch a household word in the horticultural world, for permission to reproduce photographs of rockeries constructed by his firm. The designs are amongst the best and most sensible which we have seen.

Engraving No. 40 (page 161) represents a

40. A rock garden walk (page 162).

41. Open rockery, showing a great variety of "pockets" and "compartments" (page 162).

rock garden walk. The position of the great masses of rock, their general disposition, and the provision of compartments for growing rock-loving plants of any size are all that could be desired.

Rockery on a large scale is also exhibited by picture No. 41 (page 161). Here are shown a great variety of "compartments" and "pockets" for displaying plants of almost any size. A portion of a field could be utilised, or of a large lawn adjoining a house.

The disposition of huge blocks of stone for the purpose of displaying—in the big compartments—the "carpeting" of small rock plants is exemplified in engraving No. 42 (page 163). Of course, it is obvious that the mere space occupied by these great masses of stone piled up to exhibit one phase—a most interesting one, it is true—of natural rockery would be sufficient to find room for hundreds of small plants arranged as a microcosm of Alpine scenery.

In illustration No. 43 (page 163), we have

42. Rockery suitable for the display of "carpeting" (page 162).

43. A running water scene in association with rock-loving plants (page 162).

the effect of a running water scene in association with rock-loving plants. It gives a most natural representation of what one might find not only in Switzerland, for instance, but upon our own moorlands and mountainous or hilly country. In such a rockery as this the purely aquatic plants could be utilised.

Another illustration of a water scene is given in engraving No. 44 (Frontispiece); but here the water space is larger. It only gives an example of the sort of scene which could be extemporised where abundant space is available and expense is not spared.

In our last engraving—No. 45 (page 165)—the rocky arrangement is again on a large scale; but the owner of a small garden with only space for a little bit of rockery could perhaps obtain as much enjoyment—by the study of these models and by reproducing everything that has been shown on a massive scale. The idea of the several arrangements can easily be mastered, and by giving a little play to the imagination, the microcosm

45. Rockery on a massive scale (page 164).

would afford as much pleasure as the largest rockery that could be built in the largest available space.

THE END

INDEX

Printed by W. Brendon and Son, Ltd., Plymouth

Printed in the United Kingdom
by Lightning Source UK Ltd.
128956UK00001B/159/A